INTRODUCTION TO TUNING

by
Martyn
Watkins

speed sport
motobooks

INTRODUCTION TO TUNING
First impression June 1969
Second impression February 1970
Second Revised edition November 1972
Third edition July 1974

ISBN 0 85113 002 X

ISBN 0 85113 082 8

Published by
Speedsport Motobooks
(Interauto Book Company Limited)
Bercourt House, York Road, Brentford,
Middlesex, TW8 OQP, England

Printed in Great Britain by
HGA Printing Company Ltd.,
Brentford, Middlesex

Contents

FOREWORD FOR INTRODUCTION TO TUNING

This book is number one in a series produced for the new comer to the tuning game. Unlike other titles in the Speedsport Motobook range, in this series we do not assume that the reader has the basic knowledge and experience, instead we allow for the enthusiast who is keen to learn from the beginning.

The first volume, this book, sets out to give a general picture of the principles of the various parts of the car, how they work and what they do and in general terms how they can be improved.

Volume two is devoted to tuning the engine and transmission and enlarges on the various points raised in this book so that the amateur tuner gains the fundamental knowledge of what he is doing. Volume three covers the all important subject of tuning suspension and brakes. Volume four deals with modifying production cylinder heads. Volume five is about the electrical system. Volume six goes on to the final stage, racing engine preparation. For information on the detailed tuning of specific models there are, of course, many other books in the Speedsport range with more to come.

Chapter 1.

Making a Start

Everybody has to make a start sometime, and presumably even the late Pomeroy, L. wasn't a first-class engineer as a toddler.

Any book like this which sets out to spell things simply for the beginner has to be pretty basic, and this first chapter is strictly for the real new boy. But we have to start like this because once we get on to the more detailed aspects of engine performance improvement it won't be a lot of good if some of our readers don't fully appreciate, for instance, exactly what we mean by torque. To mention but a few, as they say.

So we have to start right at the beginning, which is the modern internal combustion engine. Most of what we're trying to say covers most engines in broad principle; in some cases, particular engines differ in detail, but if you once grasp the basics, the variations should be pretty easy to follow, and that, children, is your homework.

Most people gave up the idea of single-cylinder engines for motor-cars about sixty years ago, but that doesn't alter the fact that whether you've got a four or a V-16 the whole issue is simply a multiplication of the basic single cylinder. It'll make life a lot easier to begine with if we go on looking at the engine as a single cylinder unit while we get down to principles and what makes it tick. Or rather, bang, and we can get on to some of the complexities later.

So a single-cylinder engine is really a sort of tube. It's a bit like a bicycle pump: you have a tube, in one end of which is a moveable piston which you shove in and out with the handle, and in the other end is a hole out of which air squirts when you push the handle, and therefore the piston, towards it. This is because the air is compressed, doesn't care for it any more than you would, and therefore looks for a way out. If you block up the hole, with a paper pellet, for instance, and pump the handle, you should notice two things. First, the handle movement will be a lot stiffer and you won't be able to close the pump right up until, second, the pellet flies out (with a little practice you can achieve astonishing accuracy, too). But if you bung up the hole with something that is fixed, and can't fly out, you should notice two more things as you push the piston towards the end where the hole was. First, the piston (and the handle) stops quite violently some way up the barrel of the pump, or tube, and, second, if you push sharply there will be a tendency for the piston to get shoved smartly back again.

What we've done here is to determine, very roughly, the compression ratio of the pump, because the car engine does the same thing. The piston rushes up the bore of the cylinder until the air — in this case a mixture of petrol and air — is compressed to the point at which it will compress no further. The end of the cylinder

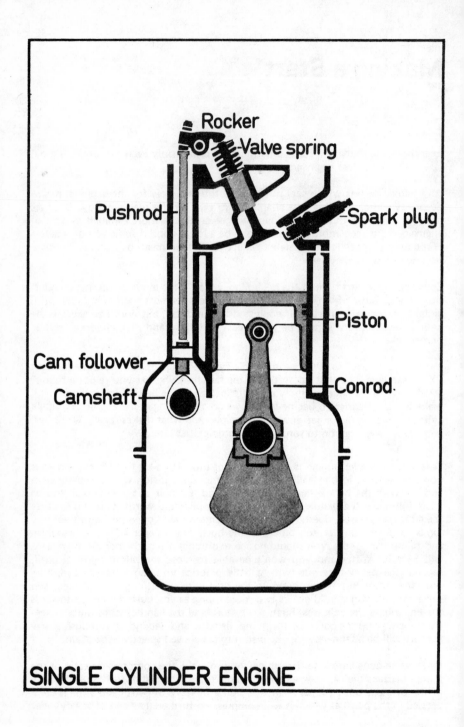

SINGLE CYLINDER ENGINE

is blocked off solidly with the cylinder head, and so the air/fuel mixture can't escape: it therefore pushes back against the piston and tries to shove the thing away, cos it hurts (probably).

At this point, let's forget about bicycle pumps and concentrate on engines. The piston is a tightish fit inside the cylinder, and we make sure that no air/fuel mixture can escape past when it is being compressed by means of piston rings, which squash out against the sides of the cylinder. This also means that air can't get into the cylinder past them, and so we have to make holes in the cylinder head. This, of course, destroys the whole object of the exercise, so we immediately proceed to fill the holes up again but this time we must make sure that we can open and close them when we want to. We do this by means of valves which are mechanically linked to the movement of the piston so that they are closed tight when the piston is moving upwards and doing its squashing bit and open when its going downwards so that more fuel/air mixture can be drawn in. We'll go into the hows and whys later. Now then. Simply squashing the fuel/air mixture and then letting it go again isn't going to give the piston much of a downwards shove. Theoretically if we squashed it tight enough it would go bang, and this is the theory of the diesel, or compression-ignition, engine — you squash the mixture so tight that it does go bang. But petrol engines don't work like this, and to give the piston a real sharp shove downwards we set fire to the fuel/air mixture; being in a confined space, it goes bang. A bang is simply a violent expansion of gas, and a violent expansion means that it wants more room. In this case, it gets more room by shoving the piston smartly down the cylinder again.

The piston, of course, is connected to a rod, called a connecting-rod (isn't it all marvellously imaginative?) and the connecting-rod can be attached to whatever we want. In the case of the car engine, it is latched onto the crankshaft, so called because it is a shaft (we'll let you know, darling) with cranks in it, cranks being (in this application) sharp bends. If we hook the con-rod onto the crankshaft at right angles any latent genius will spot the possibilities for turning vertical motion into horizontal motion, and we are Getting Somewhere.

On the internal combustion engine, all these reactions are arranged in a cycle, called the Otto cycle after the foreign gentleman who first pedalled it, about which every schoolboy, and possibly one or two schoolgirls, gets pretty blase by the time he's twelve or so. Mr. Otto, or Herr Otto if you like, got lots of pistons rushing up and down lots of cylinders and took Careful Notes, which enabled him to see that a cycle of four strokes are all put together and make the engine work. The first thing that happens is that the piston nips smartly down the bore of the cylinder and sucks in a mixture of petrol and air through the valve which, with devastating logic, is called the inlet valve. Then it nips back up again on what is called the compression stroke and, with the inlet valve closed and sealing off the end of the cylinder, compresses the mixture. At the end of this stroke, more or less, the mixture is set fire to by means of a spark at the sparking plug which has been craftily inserted at the top of the cylinder and the whole thing goes off bang. When it goes bang, it expands, so it shoves the piston smartly back down to the bottom again on what is called (you've guessed) the expansion or power stroke. The fourth stroke of the cycle is called the exhaust stroke or, scavenge, and all this does is to clear the decks so that the whole thing can happen again. The burnt gas is still in the space between piston and cylinder head, so the piston hops back up to the top, shoving the burnt gas in front of it, and as it goes another valve in the head opens (called the exhaust valve, of course) and all the muck is squirted out through it. And Bob's yer uncle (or at least, that's who Mummy says he is).

The more perceptive among you will by now have caught on the fact that this cycle can take a large share of the blame for the popularity of the four-cylinder engine. In a single-cylinder unit, all this takes a fair amount of time and the power tends to be delivered in a series of jerks. So a long time ago the motor makers decided to lash four of'em together in what they thought they'd call a cylinder block, so that you could arrange each cylinder's firing, or power stroke, to follow on the heels of the one before it and you could then get a power stroke from somewhere in the engine more or less continuously. This means that some pistons must be up while others are down, which is why the crankshaft is, er, cranked the way it is. If you simply number the cylinders one-to-four from one end, and arrange matters so that the power strokes are delivered in the same order, the effect is Nasty and the engine will fall apart. So to balance the power strokes and the stresses on the crankshaft, an order of firing, designated the firing order by the same awe-inspiring processes of thought, was worked out, which is usually 1-3-4-2.

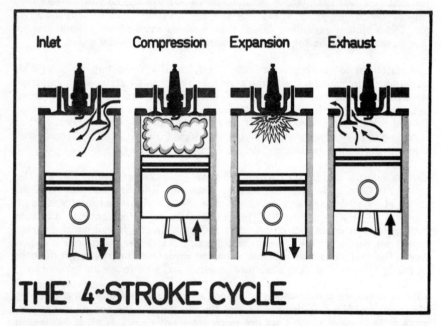

THE 4~STROKE CYCLE

Now we're getting somewhere. To recap for a moment, we've got the piston working inside the cylinder, which is housed with its mates in the cylinder block. The piston is connected to the crankshaft by means of the connecting rod, and sucks in fresh fuel/air mixture from the carburettor, which is where the fuel and air are mixed in their correct proportions, through the inlet valve. The compressed mixture is exploded by means of a spark from the sparking plug, and the burnt gas is exhausted through the exhaust valve. What makes these valves work? Basically, the camshaft does it. The camshaft is another shaft with lumps on, called lobes, and is made to revolve by being connected to the crankshaft, sometimes by a chain, sometimes by toothed gears, and sometimes, nowadays, by a toothed belt. These lobes are eccentric on the camshaft; they stick out more on one side than they do on the other, like some people's ears. It is the lobes which, either directly or indirectly by means of pushrods and things (which we'll come to later) open the valves, and because the camshaft is driven by the crankshaft the valve openings can be timed precisely according to the position of the piston within the cylinder. In most cases the cam only has to open the valve; they are left to look after their own closing problems and given springs which are compressed when the valve is pushed open by the camshaft and which snap the valve-head back on its seat as soon as the pressure comes off. The stronger the the spring, the faster the valve will be closed and the more tightly it will seat but — from the point of view of tuning — this also means that the camshaft will have to use more power to force the valve open against their pressure.

The extent to which the gas is compressed inside the cylinder is known as the compression ratio. What exactly is meant by 'compression ratio of nine-to-one' is that the gas is compressed to one-ninth of its original uncompressed volume. Broadly speaking, the more the mixture is compressed when the spark ignites it, the bigger the bang, and thus the greater the downward force on the piston and the more power there is in the power stroke. This is why a common tuning procedure is to increase the compression ratio — in other words, to compress the gas still further. But you can't go round compressing the gas infinitely — if you do, the mixture will go bang diesel-style of its own accord just because it is so tightly compressed. This may happen before the spark sets it off, a condition known as pre-ignition. This can mean that the mixture goes bang before the piston is ready for it, and a mighty explosion clobbers the piston while it's still on its way up, which is bad for it, and why pre-ignition through too high a compression ratio is a Bad Thing.

The force with which the piston is shoved down the cylinder by the bang is measured in horse-power and, on motorcars, by brake horse-power. This is the power actually available at the crankshaft and its name comes from the fact that, on the test-bed on which it is measured, a braking force is applied to measure the power. The power figure quoted in the manufacturer's literature will the maximum power which the engine will develop on full throttle — in other words, with a maximum amount of fuel/air mixture being drawn into the cylinder for compression — and at maximum revolutions. There are, commonly, two figures for this: nett, or DIN brake horse-power, is the figure achieved with the exhaust system and all the auxiliaries which have to be driven by the engine when it is installed in a car; because all these things use up some of the power for themselves, this figure is less than the gross, or SAE, horsepower figure. Modern engines are not constant speed devices, but run at varying crankshaft speeds according to load and throttle opening, or the weight of fuel/air charge drawn into the cylinder, and therefore the amount of horse-power developed will vary accordingly. At low speeds and small throttle openings, when the combustion space (that part of the cylinder in which the fuel/air mixture is compressed and explodes) is not completely filled, the brake-horsepower figure will be lower than that un-

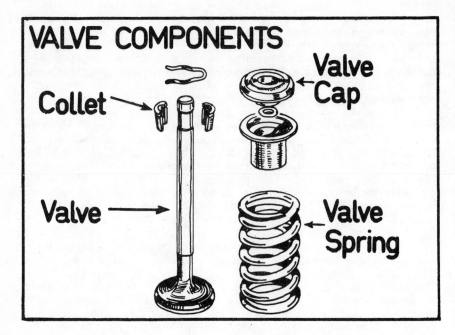

VALVE COMPONENTS

Collet

Valve Cap

Valve

Valve Spring

der maximum power conditions, and by taking readings throughout the engine's speed and throttle range the manufacturer gets what is called a power curve.

This isn't the only way of measuring an engine's capabilities: there is torque as well, and torque is probably one of the most widely misunderstood features known to science. Torque, it says in the school text-books, is a turning force, and a fat lot of good that is, It gets its name, if you're interested, from the Latin torqueo, which means to twist — well, I twist, if you must know, but that doesn't seem to get us much further. So let's forget about definitions and try explanations. Torque is really a measure of the actual expansion pressure on the pistons after the bang, and is an indication of just how hard the piston is being shoved down the bore after the bang. It is measured in foot-pounds, and is at its greatest at only one particular engine speed — usually between half and threequarters of the peak engine speed — when the combination of all the varying factors is such that the maximum possible fuel charge is being drawn in, compressed and fired to its fullest effect. As engine speed gets past this point the time the fuel/air mixture has to get itself organised obviously diminishes, and so torque tends to diminish with it above this ideal speed; the same thing happens at lower speeds because, instead of piston speed it is valve opening and closing which reduces the speed at which the mixture is moved about.

To get hold of an understanding of the design features which govern engine performance, we shall have to get hold of the relationship between horse-power and torque. Because maximum torque occurs, usually, between half and threequarters of the peak engine speed, then the higher the speed at which b.h.p. is achieved the higher, too, will be the speed at which we get our best torque figure. Also, you have to bear in mind that while brake horse-power varies according to engine speed, torque is more closely linked to engine capacity, assuming all other things to be equal: as an example of this, let's look at the well-known Ford tuner's trick of boring the 1500 c.c. Ford engine to 1650 c.c. This little exercise, carried out at considerable trouble and probably a lot of expense, gives our wizard around about eight b.h.p. more than he started with. Big deal? No, because that wasn't why he did it — he went for the significant increase in torque which is derived.

Since engine power varies according to engine speed, do we simply run our engines faster to get more b.h.p.? Up to a point, this may be true, but the theory isn't borne out in practice all the way, largely because of a phenemenon first described by Newton, who was the fellow more widely-known because of the strange things he did with apples. Friend Newton worked out the stress involved in accelerating or decelerating a given object varies as the square of the speed it reaches in a given time. So if we reckon that a conventional car engine's piston is trying to shake itself off the connecting rod to which it is attached, the force with which it is pushing and pulling every time it goes up and down is four times as great at a piston speed of 2,000 feet per minute than it is with a piston speed of 1,000 feet per minute.

So instead of making the piston rattle up and down at high speed, we can get a greater force exerted upon it by making the piston area greater, which is what our Ford chum was doing a couple of paragraphs back and which is why torque is more closely linked with capacity than speed. But there are physical limits to this, too: the weight of an object varies as the cube of its size and since the heavier the piston, the more of our engine's power we use up trying to shove it up the cylinder, there are pretty fine limitations on the use of pistons as big across as saucers.

A further limiting factor on engine speed lies in the use of the valve gear itself: if the engine speed is to high, and the piston dashes about too quickly, there will not be time to get the valves open and shut to control the flow of fuel/air mixture. This is where we go onto cylinder head design, valve timing and so on, and is a subject best left for the next chapter.

Chapter 2

Cylinder Heads, Valves and so on

The first chapter of this book mentioned the cylinder head a good deal without doing anything to dispel the illusion that this is anything more than a flat plate stuck across the top of the cylinder. It ain't of course—it's a very technical part of the whole of the engine and in most cases it is the cylinder head which is the first thing to be attacked by the engine tuner. The reason for this is a simple one: up to a point, it is the head, and the shape and size of the combustion chambers inside it, which control the performance of the engine as a whole, and other factors, such as carburation and so on, are themselves totally dependant on the combustion chamber. And it is high time, though not necessarily the best time, to introduce a note of confusion: not all engines nowadays have their combustion chambers in the head itself, although this is still the most common place to find it. But bowl in-piston engine designs, such as the crossflow Ford Cortina/Escort power units, the Rover 2000 and so on, are fitted with cylinder heads which, so far as the combustion space is concerned, are just flat metal plates, although they still have to have ports, valves and so on, and the combustion chamber is formed in the top, or crown, of the piston. These, however, are still special cases and, in any case, the question of combustion chamber and port shape is still governed by the same fundamentals no matter whether the port or chamber is in the head, the piston or, come to that, sitting on the back seat.

Let's take the combustion chamber first. This has two main jobs to do: the first, and most obvious one, is to provide somewhere for the fuel/air mixture to sit and wait until the piston comes up, shuts the door and the spark from the plug makes the whole thing go bang, forcing the door open and giving the piston a right old shove downstairs where it came from. This would be easy if, in the first place, you were going to fill the space completely with exactly the same amount of fuel/air mixture every time and, in the second place, if that's all you wanted to happen. But because the engine is a variable speed device, as we said before, you don't always shove in the same amount of fuel/air mixture—for instance, there are the extremes of idling and full-throttle operation, and every stage between. And secondly, you don't just want the burnt gas to lie there after the explosion like an unsold kipper—you want to get rid of it, fast, before the next lot of unburnt gas arrives, which at, say, 4,000 r.p.m., will be SOON.

So the gas must be in the right place at the right time, for a starter, and this is easy to arrange. But it also has to be moving in the right direction, which is not so simple. All of it must be made to move if we're going to get the best out of the engine, so that no pockets of unburnt gas remain: if they do, we aren't getting the full benefit of the explosion—the bang ain't big enough, like those fourpenny bangers we've all been disappointed in on November 5th.

Look at the explosion a bit more closely—not literally, but in your Minds. An explosion is really nothing more than a flame burning in a confined space: if you extract cordite from a cartridge, spread it on a flat surface and apply a match, the explosion will not be spectacular—in fact, you'll probably have some trouble getting the stuff to burn. But pack it all into the cartridge and the results will be a little more satisfying—you may even blow your stupid head off if you don't take our word for it. The same thing happens in the engine: the spark from the sparking plug sets fire to the fuel/air mixture and, if the combustion chamber is the right shape, the flame path will travel right through the available mixture and the whole thing will burn—and, since it is in a tightly confined space, it will go bang. So that is one factor controlling the shape of the head. Then, after the bang, we have the chamber full of burnt gas, which is not only useless, but since the chamber is already full of this there's no room left for a fresh lot of combustible mixture to move in for next time. So we've got to get rid of it, and it's in the wrong end of the cylinder simply to fall out of the hole when we open the exhaust valve. Rather than redesign the modern engine so that the combustion chamber is at the bottom, let's see how they do it, starting with what actually happens.

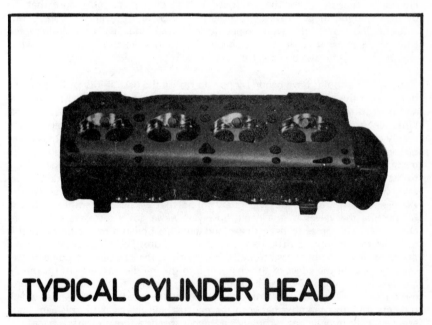

TYPICAL CYLINDER HEAD

Leaving supercharging alone for a minute, the fuel/air mixture has only got atmospheric pressure to shove it into the combustion chamber from the carburetter, and, in the same way that a flat paper bag won't fill itself up with air if you leave it lying around, this is insufficient to fill the combustion chamber on its own. The piston must therefore be called on to encourage it with a bit of a push for the exhaust and a bit of a suck for the inlet. To make the most of this, we also have to take a few liberties with the valve timing or the periods during each of the piston's strokes when the valves are open and shut. Bearing in mind that the object of the exercise, ideally, is to exhaust the burnt gas totally and completely refill the combustion chamber with unburnt fuel/air mixture, we can open the inlet valve at the start of the induction stroke, logically enough, and then keep it open until the piston is well on its way back up the bore of the cylinder for the compression stroke. At the same time, we can open the exhaust valve before the piston reaches the end of its power stroke and keep it open, not only for the upward exhaust, or scavenge stroke, but also until well after the beginning of the induction stroke. Anyone still with us will appreciate that this means that both the inlet and exhaust valves are both open at the same time, and a reasonable question is on the subject of making sure that the burnt gas and unburnt knows which door ro come in by and go out of. The answer is in combustion chamber shape. If we've got this right, the fresh charge of fuel/air mixture coming in through the inlet valve will give us a hand where its most needed to push the burnt charge out of its exhaust valve, which is desirable.

This business of keeping both valves open at the same time is called overlap, and is found to its most pronounced extent on racing engines where the overlap may have a duration of up to 70 degrees of crankshaft rotation. This is dandy at high crankshaft speeds, where the gas speed is high enough to make sure that the burnt and unburnt gases stay out of each other's way. But at low speeds—say, below 4,000 r.p.m.—this won't work quite so well, and this is the basic reason why racing camshaft profiles—the shape of the lobes which operate the valves—are not suitable for use on road cars.

You will, or should, have begun by now to realise the desirability of keeping the mixture on the move all the time it is in the chamber: this is called turbulence, and it is on turbulence that the rate and completeness of combustion depends. What we want to do is to get the mixture burning from the spark as rapidly and evenly as possible, to make sure that the whole of the charge of mixture is burnt up, and then to make sure that the residue is got rid of as quickly as possible to make room for the new charge. The most effective combustion chamber design to let all this happen is that provided by an overhead-valve layout and, in any case, side-valve engines (in which the valves are in the cylinder-block and not in the head at all) are nowadays so rarely found that we needn't bother with 'em. By putting the valves in the head, however, we've got a lot more freedom of choice when it comes to head shape, and what has boiled down to be the best is to make the chamber a little narrower than the bore. This means that when the piston is at the top of its stroke, the gas inside the chamber is going to get squashed out of the edges of the chamber into the middle, this area of maximum compression being known as a "squish" area. Further turbulence can be promoted by a feature quite commonly found in the head—a sort of nose which projects into the chamber between the exhaust and inlet valves; this can, however, actually impede gas turbulence as higher speeds although it has a beneficial effect in some cases at low speeds.

Quite obviously, it is pretty important that the chamber roof should be as smooth as possible so that the gas can "flow" over it and so that there are no projections or obstructions which can create "pockets" where unburnt gas may lurk. When an engine is being tuned, the combustion chamber roof should be polished all over to a matt finish, and this is where we might take a look at what we do to the average head when we are tuning for performance. What we have to

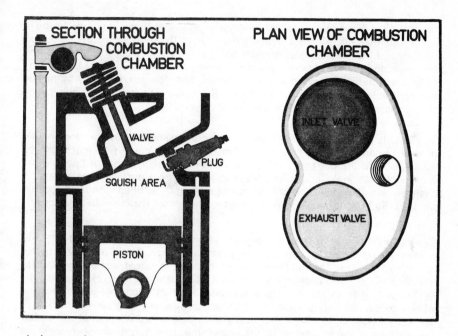

SECTION THROUGH COMBUSTION CHAMBER

VALVE

PLUG

SQUISH AREA

PISTON

PLAN VIEW OF COMBUSTION CHAMBER

INLET VALVE

EXHAUST VALVE

do is to get in as much as possible in the weight of charge of fuel/air mixture and then to compress it as much as we can within the limits of detonation, or pre-ignition. At first sight, this looks like a contradiction, because the first require-ment apparently argues a large combustion space and the second wants a small one so that the piston can compress the gas as much as possible: the more we compress the mixture, the bigger the bang when the explosion goes off. Right?

Obviously, it is necessary to strike a balance between these two requirements. Leaving aside special purposes, like racing and the special requirements of en-gines of advanced design, we are unlikely to want to raise the compression ratio of the average overhead-valve engine to much above 10 to 1 for road use: so far as the volume of the combustion chamber itself is concerned, it is only worth having one as big as you can fill—empty space in there is no good to man or beast. In practice, the two apparently different requirements are simply solved by the nature of the work you do on them. For instance, the compression ratio can be increased either by fitting pistons which have a raised, or domed, crown to them, so that they project into the combustion space and therefore squash the mixture more tightly, or by removing metal from the face of the cylinder head, thus bringing the roof of the chamber nearer to the piston crown when the piston is at the top of its stroke and thus achieving the same effect.

Doing either of these things, but especially planing metal off the head face, is going to reduce the volume of the chamber. But on the other hand, you are going to remove metal from the chamber in the process of removing all the nasty little bumps and lumps and polishing the roof, so that is going to give you back some of the lost volume. You won't get it all back, naturally; if you did, you'd be back at the standard compression ratio again, which rather misses the point of the exercise. While you're at this business of head polishing, it will be borne in upon you that not all the combustion spaces in the head are of the same volume, one of the snags of mass production. If we're going to get the best from the engine, both in terms of power and smoothness, we obviously want a bang of the same magnitude to shove down each piston, and you won't do this by having different volumes of mixture to explode. So measure the volume of the largest and increase the size of the others until they match it.

The details of these operations vary from one engine to another, and in this general discourse we can't go into them too deeply. You'll find that most of your problems are dealt with in other articles in one of the range of Speed Sport Motobooks, so look it up there. Meanwhile, we've got ourselves, we assume, a beautiful set of combustion chambers just waiting to be filled with fresh fuel/air mixture. So how do we get it in? (Not now, thank-you, darling — Daddy's busy).

Obviously, it comes in through the inlet valves, but between them and the carburetter where it all starts there are ports. In simple form, ports are merely tunnels in the head leading the gas from the inlet manifold, on which the carburetter sits, to the valves and so into the combustion spaces. Here again, the engine only has atmospheric pressure plus a bit of encouragement from the piston to get the mixture down its throat (at low engine speeds, in fact, it is probably below atmospheric pressure) and since gas velocity is what we're after we must again think in terms of shape and smoothness. For similar reasons, the same applies to the exhaust ports, which, logically, lead the burnt gas from the chamber, via the exhaust valve, to the exhaust manifold and the rest of the exhaust system. If you look at a port in section (imagine it, preferably—don't go cutting your cylinder head in half) you'll find that generally it is dimensioned in three parts, with a biggish hole at the outside, where it meets up with the manifold, a narrower waist and then enlarging again to nearly the same size as the valve seat. Ideally, its internal surfaces should be smooth, though not polished to a mirror-finish, so as to encourage gas-flow and reduce frictional resistance. The speed of the gas will be accelerated by the "waisting" of the port, and when tuning an engine it is important that, although the ports must be polished and all snags and obstructions removed, the dimensions of each part of the port relative to the others are not changed. Of course. they don't run in straight lines, but have to turn corners, and you can further improve gas-flow by making sure that these corners turn sweetly with no sharp angles in which "pockets" of gas can collect.

You'll be dead lucky if you find that your engine has a separate port per cylinder: most production engines, in the interests of cheapness of manufacture, have what are called "siamesed" ports which, like the twins of medical rarity, are joined so that in effect one port has to do the work of two. When tuning an engine for road use this isn't a matter of vital importance, but if more advanced development is being thought about then the feature will produce snags in the way of interference with the gas paths. But by the time you get to that stage you won't be reading this.

Port design, and particularly port modification, has changed completely in the past thirty years. Then, it was thought, everything should be done to induce

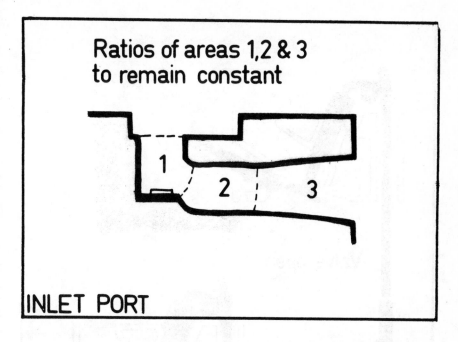

Ratios of areas 1,2 & 3 to remain constant

INLET PORT

turbulence in the gas-flow through the port, so that the fuel/air mixture could vaporise completely, with no gobs of neat petrol, while they reckoned that this also helped to equalise the distribution of mixture to each cylinder. The chap who stuck a spanner in these works was Harry Weslake, who decided that all you got from this approach was less power than if you smoothed out the path of the gas, taking into account all the projections such as valve guide bosses and so on, concentrating on moving the gas quickly along the port and getting the maximum weight of charge into the combustion space.

The direction of the port is important in playing its part in the gas movement within the combustion chamber, but this is less vital when it comes to the exhaust side. All we have to bear in mind is that the gas will go through a small hole at a higher speed than through a big one, provided that the port is large enough at its entrance to let the full burnt charge in. After that, our only concern is to get the useless muck into the exhaust manifold and out of the way.

Valves, now. We know what valves are for, and now we can look a little more closely at the inlet valve, first, and the precise job it does and how we can improve it, if possible. It is obvious that the size of the inlet valve and the length of time it stays open are major factors in the weight of mixture we can get into the combustion space. The more we can get in, assuming complete combustion, the bigger the bang and the faster the piston goes down to turn the crankshaft. This appears to suggest that its a case of the bigger, the better, where inlet valves are concerned, but this is misleading since it ignores gas velocity and turbulence. Remember that, as we said before, with a given pressure pushing it through, air goes faster through the little hole than a big 'un, and since our pressure is only

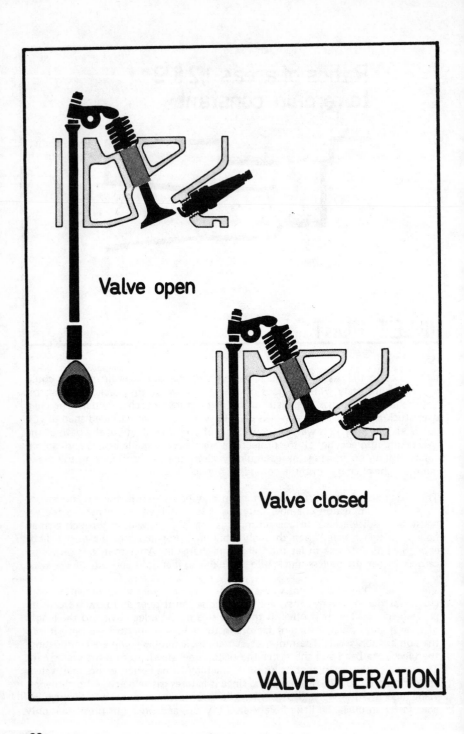

Valve open

Valve closed

VALVE OPERATION

that of the atmosphere, we actually need a smaller valve than is ideal in theory to give us good volumetric efficiency.

Increasing the size of the inlet valve up to a certain point will definitely give more power by allowing a greater weight of charge into the combustion space; above this point, we will possibly get less power because of reduced turbulence causing poor filling of the combustion space. And where it does give more power it will do so at a higher point in the engine speed range and the increase will probably be accompanied by poorer torque at lower speeds because of the reduced turbulence.

Where the exhaust valve is concerned, we have a complication: the burnt gas will be exhausted at a higher pressure than that at which it went into the combustion chamber, and it will also be darned hot. The function of the exhaust valve is two-fold: it must (obviously) act as a reliable seal for the combustion chamber, and at the same time it must be able to open sufficiently to get rid of the burnt gases as quickly as possible. What we have to try and arrange is that the valve will open quickly, so that the sudden release of pressure inside the chamber will start a rapid gas-flow down the exhaust port so that the chamber is efficiently scavenged; at the same time it has to be opened with a minimum of effort so that the engine doesn't have to use too much of its power in lifting the valve against combustion chamber pressure.

Because the burnt gas is under this pressure, it will dash out even faster through a small hole than a big 'un, and so if we use too large an exhaust valve we might find that the burnt gas was not completely scavenged because of its reduced velocity. Further, the greater the area of the valve head, the greater will be the effect of the pressure inside the chamber. Up to a point, therefore, we should keep the size of the exhaust valve as small as possible, and in most tuned engines it is left as standard even if the inlet valve is increased in size.

This question of the effort needed to open the valves takes us on to valve springs and the rest of the valve-operating gear, which includes push-rods, rockers, tappets and so forth. It also includes, indirectly, the camshaft but that is a larger subject which we'll leave for next time.

So far as the valve gear is concerned, strength has to be married up to lightness. Remember that the engine's total power output has to do its share of work in running the engine, overcoming frictional losses and above all in opening and closing the valves before you get a chance to use any of it for propelling the car. On the other hand, we want to make sure that the valves close quickly, and stay shut firmly, so a strong spring is needed. On top of that comes the question of valve bounce, which is one of the names given (it is also called valve crash, or valve float, and a number of other totally unprintable names) to a condition in which the valve remains open more or less permanently because it is pushed back open by the operating gear before the spring has had time to shut it properly. This is obviously bad for combustion chamber sealing and apart from the fact that you lose power immediately it is also a good way of destroying the valves and the valve seats. When tuning an engine it is normal to increase its maximum potential crankshaft speed because, as we said earlier, brake horse-power increases with engine speed, among other factors. So the thing to do is to fit stronger springs which will snap the valve shut even faster, but if this is overdone we shall use even more power when the valve has to be forced open against the spring pressure.

Too strong a spring also increases the loading on the rest of the valve gear which, in most engines, consists of the camshaft, push-rod, rocker and tappet. Camshafts we shall have to leave until the next chapter, as we said, except to cover the basic fact that the camshaft, driven by the crankshaft, carries on it a number of pear-shaped cams which usually operate not directly onto the push-rod but onto the base of a push-rod. As the camshaft revolves, the push-rod's foot rises up the side of the cam and the whole rod, of course, goes up with it. At the other end of the rod is a metal bar called a rocker; this is pivoted on a shaft running along the top of the engine so that as the push-rod pushes one end up, the other end bears down. It bears down, in fact, on the valve and thus pushes it open. The reason for this apparent complication is that the leverage of the rocker magnifies the movement of the push-rod or the dimensions of the cam, or both, and without it the camshaft would need to be massive. It also provides, through an extra bit called a tappet, a means of adjustment to take up the inevitable wear on the moving parts and to compensate for temperature variations in the metal which obviously cause the valve stems, push-rods and so forth to expand and contract.

Increased revolutions allow more power to be extracted from the engine and a number of other things as well: because the incoming and outgoing charges get out of each other's way more quickly, we can do clever and complicated things to the camshaft which will allow us to get still more power by getting the burnt and unburnt gases in and out more quickly still and in still greater volume. More revs also allow the car to go faster in the lower gears and, if we have enough power to reach maximum revs in top gear, in terms of maximum top speed as well. But provided we don't forget that we need extra power to flex the mighty muscles of the stronger springs, we don't necessarily need all that much extra to get a considerable improvement in acceleration times. Thus: if, by raising maximum revs, we can increase the maximum speed in second gear from, say, 55 m.p.h. to 60 m.p.h., we can improve the 0-60 m.p.h. acceleration figure because we can get to 60 without another gearchange, and since the car isn't actually being propelled for as long as it takes for the clutch-in-change-gear-clutch out routine, changing gear is a waste of time from this point of view.

Chapter 3

Camshafts, Ignition and the Bottom End

By now, presumably, we all know what the camshaft is, and what it does: if we don't, we'll assume that a shaft on which are mounted lobes, or cams, shaped like a pear which, as the shaft revolves, make the valves open and shut is a sufficient explanation.

Nowadays most engines are what are known as overhead-valve types; in other words, their valves are located in the cylinder head, above the block, rather than fitted inside the block itself, as on side-valve engines. But camshafts are still fitted in a variety of numbers and locations. The most common arrangement is to have one camshaft, located in the cylinder block and operating the valves very indirectly by means of what we discovered in the last chapter were called push-rods: this is the arrangement you find on, say, the BMC "A" series engine in the Spridget, Mini and so on, as well as on the run-of-the-mill Fords. This is the most common; it is also the easiest and cheapest for the manufacturer to produce, which is probably why it is so popular, and the head can be removed without disturbing the valve timing, but on the other hand it isn't ideal from the point of view of engine efficiency because of the enormous number of moving parts — camshaft, pushrod, rocker, and so on—involved in the valve-operating train. Obviously, all these are subject to wear and adjustment, and naturally they all add considerably to the inertia which must be overcome when the engine actually runs.

The solution to these problems is clearly to eliminate as many possible of all these moving parts so that the camshaft operates as directly on the valves themselves as is possible, allowing for the provision for adjustment and wear. So, on more modern and more efficient engine designs the camshaft finds itself moved up into the head, where the valves are, and with that death-defying logic we've come across before, engineers and other clever chaps have decided that, since the camshaft is now above the engine mass, it had better be called an overhead camshaft. We've still only got one overhead camshaft, and so, ruthlessly, they call it a single camshaft. Astonishing, but listen to this: when there are two of 'em, they call it a twin-overhead camshaft engine. Incidentally, such engines as the Vauxhall 1600 and 2-litre, the Hillman Imp, and so on are single overhead-camshaft engines, while the best-known examples of the twin-overhead layout are probably the Jaguar and the Lotus-Ford "Twin-Cam".

Of course, it's no good the camshaft whistling round and round slamming valves open and shut in any old order: the whole thing has to be arranged according to the principles of the four-stroke cycle and the firing order of the engine, both of which we discussed in part one. The order in which the valves open and shut, and the length of time they stay open and shut, are both controlled by the position of the cams on the camshaft, and by the shape of the camlobes themselves. The camshaft itself is driven either by a chain or, as on say the Vauxhall, or Fiat engines, by a toothed belt from the crankshaft so that it runs at a speed which is constantly related to engine speed—about half crankshaft speed is usual. In standard form, as the engine leaves the factory, the designer knows that it is going to be called on to carry out a wide range of work and therefore provides a valve timing which is going to be as versatile as possible when related to the characteristics of the engine in question. It probably won't give a very impressive absolute maximum b.h.p. figure, and it probably won't deliver all the torque that the engine is capable of, but it will provide a respectable value in both cases and, in general terms, any departure from this timing, although it can give you an improvement in one respect or the other, will probably be accompanied by poorer figures in whatever is the ignored direction and also, in some cases, by increased wear and tear. For instance, if we take a highly-tuned BMC "A" series engine in a racing Mini, it will almost certainly be fitted with the racing camshaft known as the BMC 649. This cam profile provides maximum b.h.p. at a higher engine speed than before, but because of the long period of overlap, when both inlet and exhaust valves are open together, it will deliver very little low-speed torque, and probably insufficient to keep the car moving at, say, less than 3,000 r.p.m. In addition, because of the violent movement imparted to the push-rods and valves by the steep cam profiles, valve-gear wear will be very high—a few hundred miles only, perhaps, will elapse before the whole bang shoot needs to be replaced.

So auntie, basically, needs a camshaft which will provide, in a given engine, bags of low-speed torque and she probably doesn't care much about the b.h.p. figure at seven-five: likely she'll never see seven-five anyway. Meanwhile, our ace hero of the circuits is only concerned with maximum b.h.p., and if there's no torque below five thousand, much he should worry. Obviously the same camshaft profile won't suit 'em both, but the factory engine designer has had to try and find a profile and timing which will keep 'em both reasonably happy. If you think a change of camshaft would be the answer to your car's lack of perform-ance, the first thing to do is to work out what you want to do. If you use the thing mainly as a commuter hack, which has to start readily, run smoothly at all speeds from flat-out to prolonged idling in a traffic snarl-up, you want a touring camshaft. If, on the other hand, the car is a competition machine with no shop-ping use at all, then the racing profile is going to suit you better. The difference between racing and touring cams is a threefold one, lying in the total amount of lift given to the valve, the speed at which the valve is opened and the rate, there-fore, at which it is accelerated, and, finally, the length of time the cam holds the valve in the open position, known as the "dwell". All these things are governed by various parts of the cam lobe: the amount of lift is provided by the heel of lobe, and the rate of acceleration of the valve is governed by the curvature of the shoulders. The dwell period is controlled by the shape of the lobe nose. In other words, a touring cam, giving limited lift, gradual acceleration and limited dwell for short overlap, will have the heel of the cam quite close to the shaft itself. The shoulders will be well rounded so that the valve stem, or interposed valve gear, climbs gradually up to the nose; the nose itself will, on very touring cams, be almost pointed so that dwell is very short—the valve climbs up the shoulder gradually and then, quickly, falls over the tip of the nose and starts going down again. A racing cam, on the other hand, will have a pronounced heel, very steep shoulders and an almost flat nose for prolonged dwell.

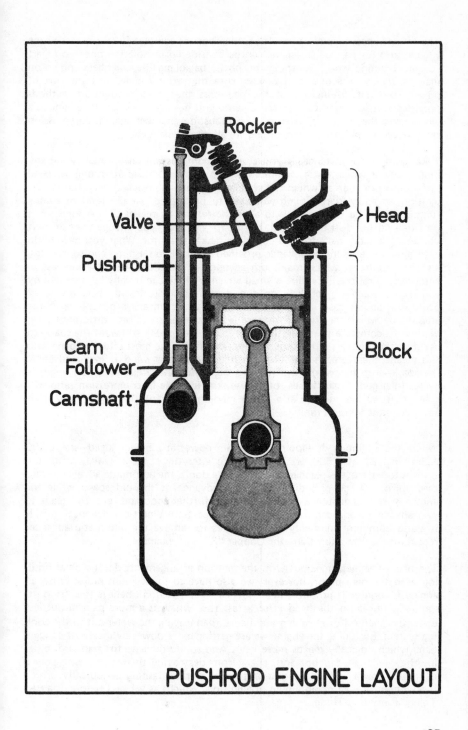

Rocker

Head

Valve

Pushrod

Cam
Follower

Camshaft

Block

PUSHROD ENGINE LAYOUT

The effectiveness of any camshaft profile depends completely on the rest of the engine, and no part of an engine can be considered in isolation once you start advanced tuning work. Polishing the ports, balancing the chambers and so on may be dandy as a means of making sure that your engine gives the sort of power it ought to instead of the near-miss that mass production methods provides, but for significant improvements you have to consider the engine as a whole, and the camshaft, valve sizes, combustion chamber shapes, compression ratio, manifolding and ignition timing are all inter-dependent.

Take ignition, for instance. If you alter the compression ratio, or carry out any modifications which cause maximum power to be produced at an engine speed different from that at which the standard power unit reached peak b.h.p., the ignition advance/retard timing will have to be altered. At the level of simple tuning, it will be O.K. merely to alter the setting by means of the adjustment provided on the distributor head, but if, for instance, you change the camshaft you will probably have to fit a complete new distributor. What you have to do is to alter the amount of advance provided at maximum r.p.m., and sometimes, also, the r.p.m. at which maximum advance is provided. A simple increase in compression ratio will require a small advance which can usually be provided by winding on a few "clicks" on the distributor adjustment, because—fairly obviously—an increase in compression ratio, which means a difference in the amount by which the fuel/air mixture is compressed, requires a different length of time to complete the operation that it did before. We still want the spark to occur at the moment of maximum compression, for the most effective bang, and this means, therefore, that we need it a little earlier than we did. So we 'advance' the spark—in other works, we make it happen a shade earlier in the engine's cycle. In a good many cases, of course, the increase in compression ratio will mean that we have to run at a higher grade of fuel, and this also will want an advance in the ignition timing.

Where the engine is developing maximum power at a higher speed—say, 6,500 r.p.m. instead of 5,500—we shall have to alter the point at which maximum distributor advance is reached, because if we don't, the automatic advance/retard mechanism will be providing maximum advance at the old speed while the engine tries to encourage it to go on for a further thousand revs: this leads to over-advancing, and can cause a lot of damage. So it Won't Do. To check this, it is quite common on highly-tuned engines to remove the automatic advance/retard mechanism altogether—the Cooper "S" is an example.

The necessary messing-about with the ignition arrangements don't stop at fiddling with the distributor, however—we also have to think about plugs. When an engine is running it produces heat—lots of it: if you don't believe this, try putting your finger on the head after a fast run, which is a more painful but less expensive method of checking the theory than leaving the water out of the cooling system. By tuning tne engine we are getting more power by means of a bigger bang which, logically means more heat. And so, if you leave the standard plugs in, they will get too hot and, apart from destroying themselves, will glow a delightful cherry red all the time instead of merely flashing periodically, which is a wonderful way of obtaining pre-ignition. Which, as we said before, is a Bad Thing, a very Bad Thing.

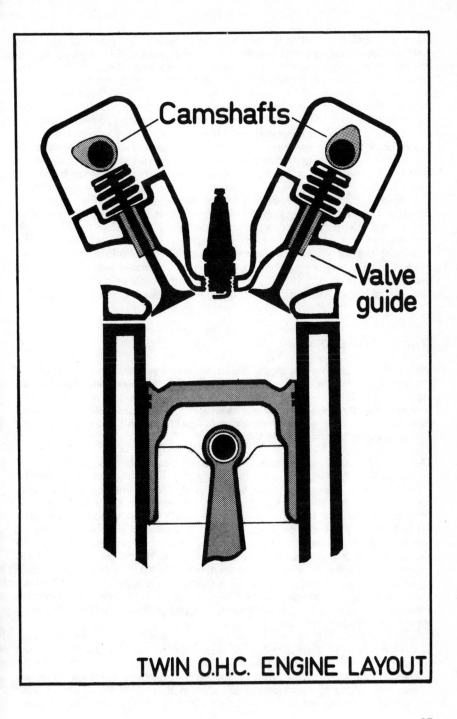

Camshafts

Valve guide

TWIN O.H.C. ENGINE LAYOUT

Plugs are graded according to their heat range, and if the right heat range plug isn't chosen you won't get the right sort of performance. Even without expensive pre-ignition you'll get misfiring, poor starting, poor idling and so on. The varying grades are loosely called "hot" and "cold", or soft and hard, a description which has damn-all to do with the heat of the spark but which refers to the rate at which the plug transfers heat away from the firing end. One which does so slowly, so that the firing end remains hot, is, reasonably, called a hot plug, while a cold one is the chap that gets rid of heat as quickly as possible and remains cold—relatively speaking, of course. If the temperature in the combustion chamber are likely to be higher than normal, as they are if you have tuned the engine, you will need a colder, or harder, plug. This is governed by several factors which include a higher compression ratio, weak carburation mixture, advanced ignition timing, supercharging, competition motoring, where full throttle operation is maintained for longish periods, and so on. You can get a rough idea of whether or not your plugs are O.K. for the job in hand by checking them after a run, switching off the engine at full power and coasting to a standstill without allowing the engine to idle or over-run. Whip out the plugs and have a shufti at the firing ends: if the plug end is coated with light brownish deposits, you're alright. If it has gone white, with no deposits at all, the plug is too hot; dry black deposits, or wet, oily ones, indicate that the plug is too cold.

THE BOTTOM END

We've left the bottom-end of the engine, by which we mean the crankshaft and its associated bearings, the connecting-rods and the flywheel, until now because, apart from making sure that it is in good condition, there isn't very much which can be done by the tuner without redesigning the complete power unit; until you reach the stage of fairly advanced tuning, there isn't, either, a great deal which needs to be done in general terms.

Any engine, tuned or standard, leaves a good deal to be desired in terms of smoothness of running, and this—apart from that part of the lack of smoothness associated with basic design—can be improved. Four-in-line engines with three main bearings for the crankshaft are less smooth than those with five; six-cylinder engines are smoother still, and a good V8 is as smooth as a turbine. There's nothing you can do about that, but you can make any engine a helluva lot better from this point of view than it is when it leaves the factory. For a start it makes even a standard car nicer to drive, while if you are going in for any tuning work, however mild, it is at least desirable that the power unit should have as much roughness eliminated as is possible. In the first stages of tuning a lot of the basic roughness will have been cured by balancing the combustion chambers, equalising their filled volumes and thus making sure that each bang is of the same magnitude as the last.

The next step is to make sure that all these identical bangs do the same amount of work. If, for instance, one connecting-rod is appreciably heavier than the others (which is not unlikely) then it follows that the bang which kicks that one about won't have so much energy left over as the others. So all the con-rods should be balanced, not only against each other, so that as near as dammit they

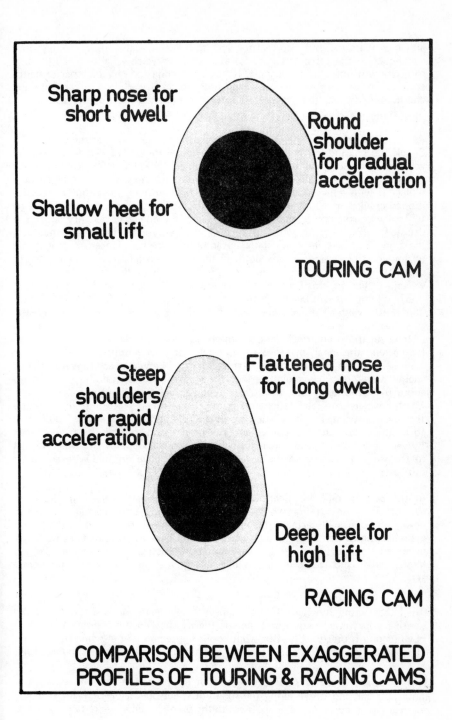

Sharp nose for
short dwell

Round
shoulder
for gradual
acceleration

Shallow heel for
small lift

TOURING CAM

Steep
shoulders
for rapid
acceleration

Flattened nose
for long dwell

Deep heel for
high lift

RACING CAM

COMPARISON BEWEEN EXAGGERATED
PROFILES OF TOURING & RACING CAMS

all weigh the same, but also end for end, so that the small end, where the rod is connected to the piston, is not, for example, appreciably lighter than the big-end, where it joins the crankshaft. If you are tuning for very high performance, such as on a racing engine, then you must select new rods very carefully and check, in addition, that the eyes at small and big ends are properly concentric. Such is mass-production that they won't always be so.

At the same time as all this work is going on, have a good look at the crankshaft. Check the bearing journals for truth, and if any are worn   decide on exactly what sort of results you might be after. If you are building up any kind of racing engine, throw the crankshaft away if the journals show any wear at all, and replace it with a new one—never, for high·power outputs, a reground or recond-itioned crankshaft. On the other hand, if you are only going in for mild tuning for a livlier road performance, then a reground one may do very well. The decision will have to be yours, though. And when you've made your mind up, the crankshaft had better be statically and dynamically balanced so that it sets up no vibration periods at any point in the engine speed range you are going to use. This requires special equipment and isn't something you can do yourself. As we said earlier on, this isn't exactly necessary on all engines for mild tuning, but nearly all engines will benefit from it and in some cases—the BMC 1100 is one— it is pretty valuable if you are only going in for a very small power increase.

Of course, the strength of the bottom end is very important when it comes to tuning, and the ideal, in terms of four-cylinder power units, is one with five main-bearings, so that the crankshaft is supported between each big-end. If your engine hasn't got five main.bearings there is, of course, nothing you can do about it. In the same way, if you're tuning for high power outputs a crankshaft which has been specially toughened by a process called "nitriding" is really the the one you want, but if no such crank is available for your engine you'll have to make do with the one you've got. Both crank and rods can be strengthened by various processes, and this is probably worthwhile, but by the time you get to the stage of serious engine development you'll have finished with advice of this sort.

In the case of the three-bearing engines—still the most common in the four-cylinder field—any tuning which is going to involve an appreciable increase in power or r.p.m. will certainly mean that it is desirable to strengthen the centre main-bearing, which is the one which will really have to do some hard work, by means of a support strap—this is very common practice on, for instance, tuned Minis, and in such cases gives a remarkable increase in crankshaft life expect-ancy!

Then there's the flywheel. If the engine is to be balanced, as it should, you're wasting your time if you don't include the flywheel in the operation, a pretty obvious point, presumably. But what about lightening it? Let's first have a look at what the flywheel is for. Think of a stationary single-cylinder engine again.

This is usually a pretty slow-revving sort of device and if you shoved such a thing in a car and drove along the road you'd get one bang—or firing-stroke— about every hundred yards or so. More to the point for what we're talking about is the fact that you'd also proceed down the road in a series of jerks because you'd only got one power stroke to every two engine revolutions. So you fit a darn great heavy flywheel whose inertia keeps the whole thing rolling in between and smoothes out the engine's revolutions. The purpose of the flywheel is. to store the energy and drive the pistons over the idle strokes, a bit like the movement of a watch.

With a four-cylinder engine, however, we've got two power strokes for every revolution of the crankshaft, and with a six-cylinder engine, three, so we can get away with a lighter flywheel. Ideally, we also want a lighter flywheel, since in doing its job it must absorb a little of the engine's power—ideally, that is, if all we're interested in is power. The lighter we can get it, within limits, the more we shall be able to improve the car's acceleration, we shall get a sharper response to the throttle, and since the engine, left to its own devices, will accelerate and decelarate more quickly than if we first had to stop or get moving a ponderous great chunk of iron, we can make much faster gearchanges as well which is a valid point for competition work.

On the other hand, we shall seriously reduce the car's ability to tick-over, it will be less smooth at low r.p.m. and it won't be so flexible. The actual power gain through lightening the component is practically microscopic and is only important on the track when every last fraction of power counts. So we might as well admit it: lighten the flywheel, and balance it, for competition; for road use, just balance it—if you lighten it under these conditions you'll really lose more than you'll gain.

Chapter 4

Carburation, Manifolding and Exhaust Systems

There are as many angles and variations on this subject as a kipper has bones, and all we can do here is to gloss over it so that, at least, we can hope to get hold of some grasp of the fundamentals. The details vary enormously from one engine to another, not only according to the rest of the specification but also on apparently identical engines. Which is why you can never give more than an approximate guide to the question 'What carburetter needle do I need for a so-and-so?'

In the early part of this book, and since, we have kept on about fuel/air mixtures and so forth, without actually going into it any more than that. This is where the carburetter comes in — it is the 'gasworks' in which fuel from the car's tank and air from the — well, from the air — are drawn together and mixed into the appropriate proportions. The snag is that there is no one appropriate proportion — an engine's requirements vary over the whole range of its performance according to temperature, speed and throttle opening. For instance, at a constant throttle opening to give a road-speed of, say, 50 m.p.h. the carburetter has to adjust the fuel/air mixture and, in fact, the flow of mixture into the combustion chamber will be small at this speed and the amount of petrol in the mixture certainly won't be great. But then look at starting the engine from cold: in the case of a simple carburetter, the sort of thing you might find on a small outboard motor, or a lawn-mower engine, you answer the engine's need for a supply of almost neat petrol, with practically no air, by sliding a shutter, usually called a strangler across the air intake so as to close it almost completely. The car's carburetter, of whatever type, is a shade more sophisticated than this, but the principle is the same.

So, just to meet these requirements, the carburetter — let's forget about fuel injection for a minute, which is simply another way of achieving the same object — has to be clever enough to vary the proportion of fuel to air from a mixture of about one-to-one for cold starts, to around five-to-one with the engine running cold, and then up to as low as 15-to-1 at the engine's economical cruising speed. Acceleration, hillclimbing and deceleration with the engine being over-run will cause further variations. And the poor old carburetter has not only got to look after the varying of these mixtures, but also has to convert them into a vapour, splitting up the fuel into tiny droplets which are suspended in the air and injected into the combustion chambers by way of ports and valves as a fine mist.

What it needs, then, is to combine a means of regulating the amount of fuel flowing through with a means of regulating the amount of air: in a simple carburetter, this is achieved by means of a throttle, to regulate the quantity of mixture passing into the combustion chamber, and a choke which can limit the amount of air available. The more sophisticated carburetters we have to deal with also control air supply by means of a system of compensating jets, which we'll come to later on.

The basis of the carburetter is the venturi, or choke tube, which in essence is a short tube which gets narrow about the waist and then returns to its original diameter. When air flows through it, the constriction at the waist causes it to accelerate, which takes us back to the earlier point we made when we said that a given quantity of air will go through a small 'ole faster than a big 'un. Right? Now then, into the narrowest part of the venturi we stick a small tube so that it projects at right angles to the air flow, and let the petrol flow continuously into this tube, taking it from a reservoir which is maintained at atmospheric pressure. When the air starts to move along the tube — because, say, the tube is connected to the cylinder of the engine in which the piston is moving on the induction stroke and therefore is sucking air through, a partial vacuum will be formed in the cylinder and similarly, in the choke tube. Nature, some wag of great wisdom is reported to have said, abhors a vacuum and immediately dials 999 or whatever is necessary to fill it, and so air rushes along the tube, goes even faster through the waist, which is where it passes over the top of the petrol inlet pipe. So in addition to drawing in air from the open end of the choke tube, it will also draw petrol out of the petrol pipe. The two will get mixed together and are drawn into the cylinder as one. Bingo, you've got mixture.

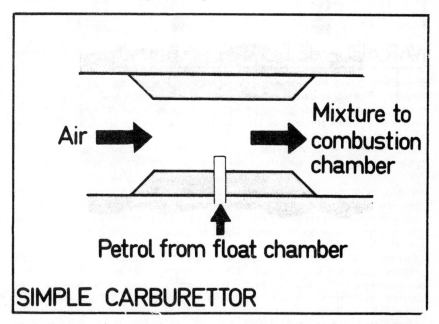

SIMPLE CARBURETTOR

But this, of course, means that, even if we introduce a flap in the choke tube, which we might as well call a throttle, to control the volume of mixture drawn into the cylinder (and thus to regulate the speed of the engine) the proportions of petrol and air int he mixture ares, so far, the same. So the dead simple carb.we have been on about until now has to grow up and get next to itself, or it'll get fired. What we need, therefore, is either a variable petrol supply or a variable air supply. There isn't much to be gained by having both except expense, and so carburetters fall into two main categories: there are those like the S.U. and the

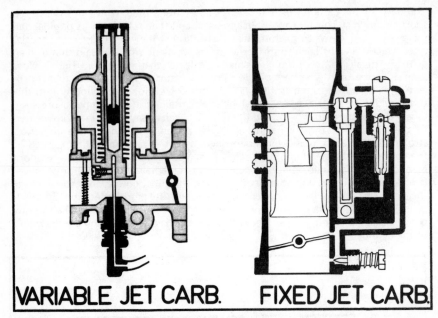

VARIABLE JET CARB.   FIXED JET CARB.

Stromberg CD, in which the air velocity over the jet is almost constant and the amount of petrol is varied by means of a tapered needle which reduces or increases the effective size of the jet by sliding up and down inside it. Then there are those in which the size, or effective size, of the petrol jet remains the same and the air supply is varied by means of those compensating jets we were talking about earlier on. The two types — and here's that awe-inspiring logic and stupefying reasoning again — are known as variable-jet and fixed jet-carburetters.

In the case of the variable-jet carburetters, such as the S.U. and the CD Stromberg, the size of the choke and the size of the jet are varied atuomatically. What happens, broadly speaking, is this. The petrol is supplied to the jet, coming from the atmospheric-pressure reservoir which on any carburettor, is the float-chamber, the function of the float being to control the level and stop the reservoir overflowing when the supply of petrol pumped from the tank is greater than the amount consumed by the engine. The petrol is supplied to the jet, as we were saying before that interruption, and the effective size of the jet governed by a tapered needle which slides up and down in its as we said before. The needle's top is fitted in the centre of a disc working in the dashpot and in which it is fitted to a suction disc, or diaphragm in the case of the Stromberg. The area above the piston in the dashpot is connected to the choke, so that the movement of air caused by the partial vacuum in the venturi also affects the piston or diaphragm. When conditions demand more petrol, the piston is sucked up inside the dashpot; as it goes it takes with it the needle, of course, drawing it up out of the petrol jet and thus increasing the effective diameter of the jet by the simple process of blocking-up less of the hole. The bottom of the piston sticks out into the choke tube, from which you can see that it therefore varies the size of the choke and if you remember, therefore the speed of the air through the venturi and over the

34

jet. Since the depression, or vacuum, over the jet is governed by the air velocity the proportion of petrol to air is then automatically sorted out. Simple, isn't it?

Fixed jet carbs., on the other hand, are a bit more complex. Leaving out all the filters and so on, what happens here is this: petrol from the float-chamber flows through a main jet and a compensating jet and on to a common channel in an emulsion block, which projects into the venturi at its narrowest point and incorporates what was, in our simple carb., the main discharge outlet into the venturi. As the throttle is opened, the resulting depression will be concentrated on this main outlet from the emulsion block, sucking petrol out. This petrol comes from the main jet through the main channel in the emulsion block and the slow-running jet (which takes a slightly different path) which has provided sufficient petrol to meet the requirements of the engine at idling speed. There is also a tube which holds petrol and which is at the moment supplying it, but as the throttle is opened further the tube, called in some cases the capacity tube, empties: its end is open to the atmosphere and so air is now fed into a compensating jet. As the throttle is opened still further, the fuel coming through the main jet meets emulsified petrol from the compensating jet in the emulsion block and this tends to break up the main jet petrol, so that more complete vaporisation takes place.

How does the petrol get to the float-chamber? In the old days, and on some motor-cycles, small outboard motors and so on, gravity is the answer. Where this isn't good enough, and you can see this on vintage racing cars, air pressure was used, a hand-pump being used to pressurise the fuel tank and thus force the fuel out. Nowadays, however, the petrol pump is the answer — presumably we all know that.

Carburetters have to be connected to the porting arrangements in the head, which is where the inlet manifold is concerned. There isn't much you have to know about these at this stage, except that, as in all cases, the flow of fuel/air mixture from carburetter to port must be smooth and as uninterrupted as possible. For this reason we try to avoid rightangled bends and steps, and when the manifold is fitted, make sure that the outlet holes mate up exactly with the port apertures in the head. The basic design of the manifold will, of course, be governed by the layout of the ports in the head, and only the length of the branches from head face to carb. mouth will be variable. In this case, most purposes require a short path, since every time the throttle is closed the mixture charge will slow down, only to be forced to accelerate again when the throttle is re-opened. This means that a snap throttle opening from low-speed, the sort of thing that continually happens on the road, is best catered for by a short path, although racing conditions may demand a different approach. The snag here is that if the mixture is heated before it reaches the combustion chambers, it will increase in volume but not in weight. In other words, the amount of air contained in the manifold will be less if it is warm, and less weight will be drawn into the cylinders, and so you'll get less power. Q.E.D. On the other hand, you will get increased flexibility. So while the road engine wants its air reasonably warm for flexibility, absolute power argues a manifold as cold as possible. The longer the pipes the greater chance the heat from the head will have to radiate away; the shorter the pipe, the opposite is true.

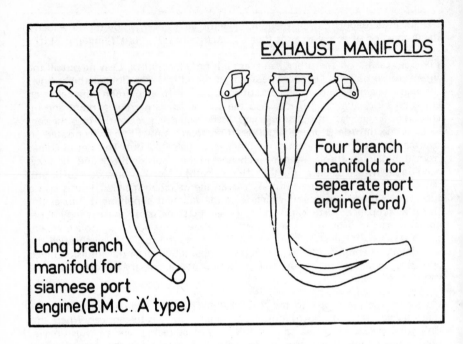

EXHAUST MANIFOLDS

Four branch manifold for separate port engine(Ford)

Long branch manifold for siamese port engine(B.M.C. 'A' type)

Now then, how many carburetters? For maximum efficiency, the answer is a carburetter per inlet port: for instance, the four-cylinder twin-cam Lotus-Ford engine with four inlet ports, operates with a carburetter, or at least a pair of twin-choke carbs (which amounts to the same thing) so arranged that each port gets its own choke and mixture supply. Siamesed-port engines make this a bit difficult to arrange, however, and in any case most people, unless they are building a fullrace engine, find they get satisfactory results from the usual compromise. What you must try and do is to cut out the long inlet manifold passages and get the carburetters close up to the ports. In most cases, this will argue two carburetters. The difficulty with a single carburetter, even if it is sufficiently large to provide the same weight of charge as two instruments, is in the varying lengths which are difficult to escape from in the inlet manifold. What this means effectively is that the two cylinders nearest to the carb. may get their charge of mixture in half the time it takes to feed those furthest away, and in extreme cases, you might get the number three cylinder receiving two supplies to every one for number four.

So much for theory, in practice, there is no doubt that on some engines — and the BMC "A" series as fitted to the Mini is an example — a large single carburetter will give as good a result as two smaller ones. The thing to do is to be bold and experiment, or to be cautious and follow the example of others. But apart from anything else, what is certain is that a modified cylinder head, with enlarged ports and bigger inlet valves, will definitely need a larger carburetter or, at the very least, a larger main jet to provide the increased amount of fuel-air mixture wich the improved breathing system will need.

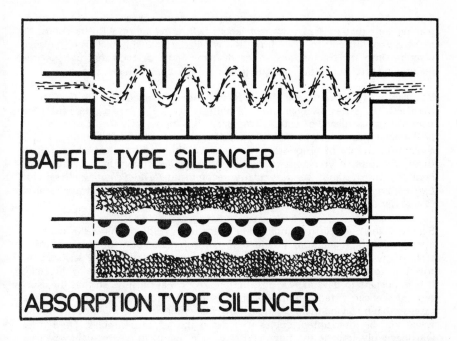

BAFFLE TYPE SILENCER

ABSORPTION TYPE SILENCER

As we said earlier there is no sense in going to all this trouble to get more fuel/air mixture into the cylinder for a bigger, better bang if we don't take some trouble to get all the unburnt gas out again. Exhaust system design is another subject on which whole books get written, and so again, we shall have to settle for basics.

Obviously, we can't hope to get complete filling of the combustion chambers with fresh fuel/air mixture if the chambers are still partly filled with exhaust residue. This has all got to be extracted. The normal exhaust system may do this very well — the situation is a bit different from the inlet side, where atmospheric pressure is all we've got to help us. When the exhaust valve opens after the bang, there is considerable pressure inside the combustion chambers and it takes a lot to stop the exhaust gases from sprinting out of a well-designed chamber. But they can't all get out by themselves. They need help, and the help we can give them is to make use of the extraction effect of the gas-flow from each cylinder. This is where manifold design is important. It is possible, if we don't keep the gas moving briskly, for interference to take place between cylinders which exhaust into the same manifold. In other words, exhaust gas from one cylinder runs into some of that left behind when the previous cylinder exhausted. Thus it is trapped in the manifold, and may get drawn back into another cylinder, an effect caused by pressure build-up in the manifold which occurs when yet a third cylinder starts to exhaust, shoves out a load of gas under pressure which promptly pushes all before it. The gas which is there to start with looks for an easy way out and if there's an open exhaust valve hard by, with nothing coming out because that cylinder has virtually finished exhausting, it nips in there out of the way.

The ideal remedy for this is to have a separate branch pipe from each cylinder, making sure that it is of sufficient length before joining up with its chums to make it very difficult for back-flow, as it is called, to take place. This brings pipe diameter into the calculations — the diameter must be such that gas speed is maintained after the initial impetus given by the piston's exhaust stroke.

You can get somehwere near this ideal even with a siamesed-port engine, such as the BMC "A" series, by giving extra length to the centre exhaust pipe from the siamesed ports. Ideals, of course, whether it is a matter of exhaust pipe lengths or diameters, can often be difficult to achieve in the space available, but there is a plentiful supply of proprietary manifolds on the market, all of which follow these principles. If you want to make a more detailed study, there are plenty of books about it, and we particularly recommend *"The Scientific Design of Exhaust and Intake Systems"*, by Philip H. Smith (whose work used to appear in *Cars & Car Conversions*).

Silencers, then. A recent complicating factor in this side of things has been the introduction of regulations intended to control the amount of noise we make and, in any case, the type of silencer used isn't going to make a very serious contribution to the engine's ultimate power output. But as in all things in this field, it is important to have as few obstructions to flow as possible, so that the usual type of silencer, fitted with internal baffles intended to break up the flow of the gases so that by giving them different flow characteristics, the free flow of sound waves will be interrupted, comes well down the list of desirables. The baffles will inevitably impede the flow, and as carbon builds up on them they will restrict things even more. A better type from the point of view of performance is the absorption-type silencer, in which the gas has unrestricted flow through a central passage which is perforated and packed in sound-absorption material to absorb the sound-waves. Carbon, again, blocks up the holes, of course, but this doesn't interfere with the gas-flow and the only complication you run into here is the matter of noise.

It is possible to get hold of any number of clever-looking gadgets to stick on the end of the tail-pipe and some loud claims are made for them. There is no doubt that those of them which have been properly designed and which are well-made can have a benefical effect, if sometimes pretty small, on engine performance. These usually operate on principles concerned with the self-extracting effect of the airstream created by the car's movement, by reducing the gas temperature or by introducing air from the atmosphere. As we said, those which are properly designed can have a worthwhile effect, but the fact remains that too many of them are merely intended to be pretty or to fool the chap with a similar car that yours is something special.

Suspension, Wheels, Tyres and Brakes

The basic reason why cars have suspension, instead of simply having the wheels bolted to the chassis, is to absorb road shocks and insulate the chassis and body, of the car against bumps. If the suspension didn't work, the whole thing would shake itself to pieces. However, there's a lot more to it than that, and from the suspension characteristics we expect to get roadholding, cornering power and, to some extent, the effective transmission to the road of the driving power of the engine and the stopping power of the brakes.

Once upon a time it was all very easy. You simply attached a beam axle at each end of the chassis, joining it by means of semi-elliptic leaf springs (cart-springs) and added some simple friction dampers. If the body rolled about too much, it was likely to bring the wheels off the ground as well, so you screwed up the dampers a bit tighter. For sporting roadholding, you stiffened up the suspension until it was pretty near rock-hard, and the twisting and flexing of the chassis took care of the difficult bits. It's all different now, of course: the modern car with monocoque construction is much more rigid than they used to be and the suspension has to provide all the answers. This, of course, is just as it should be, but it has led to greater complexity in suspension systems and while most people can appreciate that, for improved roadholding, you lower the suspension and fit stiffer dampers, not all of them are very clear as to exactly why this should be so.

Before we go into that—and more besides—let's think about the part which suspension plays in the car's performance. Leaving aside consideration of the overall speed limit which applies in this country (or had you forgotten?) it is fair to say that straight-line high speed has only very little effect on the car's average speed for a given A-B journey. Leaving motorways out of it for a moment, the difference between the highest speeds attained by, say, a Jaguar "E"-type and a Ford Cortina GT on a journey from, say, Colchester to Bristol might easily not be more than 20 m.p.h., despite that fact the Jaguar is around 60 m.p.h. faster in terms of maximum speed. Average speeds are much more largely determined by the distance on such a journey over which the two cars would be travelling at well below top speed—the corners. The important factors are the braking before the corner, the acceleration out of the corner and the actual speed through it, and all these are determined more by roadholding, and thus suspension, than by engine power.

Braking is a slightly separate subject, which we'll come to in a minute. The suspension plays its biggest part in its effect on roadholding, in which it combines with tyres. The essential thing about this combination is that the two are inter-dependent, to a great extent: poor suspension design can't be fully compensated for by tyres, and the very best of tyres are to a great extent at the mercy of the suspension characteristics.

This isn't the place to go into the intricacies of suspension design, because most of us are stuck with what we've got and very few amateur tuners are likely to be in a position to start from scratch in this field. So let's not get ourselves involved in any arguments about independence, spring rates and so on, but concentrate on getting hold of a grasp of the basic principles of roadholding and having a look to see what we can do about improving that on the car we've got. The most common from of car suspension is still the independent-front, live-axle-rear layout with coil springs at the front and, usually semi-elliptic leaf-springs behind.

This is the set-up found on most Fords, Vauxhalls and so on; Hillman Imps, most of the Standard-Triumph range and some Fords have all-independent layouts, while the BMC Mini/1100 has an all-independent system which works through a rather unusual medium. This doesn't matter—all these different systems are controlled by the same basic principles.

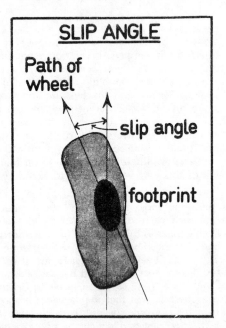

SLIP ANGLE

Path of wheel

slip angle

footprint

Roadholding is a question of stability first and foremost, and stability is governed by what is called understeer and oversteer. To get hold of exactly what is meant by these descriptions, we shall have to think about slip angles which, if you like, are a measure of the cornering power at your disposal. When you turn a corner, centrifugal force starts an argument about it and tries to insist that you go straight on. To counteract this, the tyre gets a side-thrust from the road surface—it also stops the car from slithering down into the ditch on a steeply cambered road. In doing this, the plane of the wheel makes an angle with the path along which it is travelling so that the wheel is in fact moving in a sort of semi-crabwise fashion. No loss of adhesion is necessarily involved, of course, but as the wheel revolves the contact patch, or footprint as it has come to be called, is slightly displaced every time in relation to the centre of the wheel hub. This displacement, or the angle between the plane of the wheel and the path along which it travels, is called the slip angle.

Got it? Right then. Think of a car running along the motorway with a strong cross-wind blowing. Because of the side-thrust of the wind, all four wheels will be running at slip angles. If that at the front is less than that at the rear, the car will start to turn into the wind. In effect this will be the same as if you started to turn a corner, and you will immediately have the slip angles increasing because you now have to face the problem of centrifugal force to supplement the side-thrust of the wind. The greater slip-angle at the rear will become even greater relative to the lesser angle at the front, so that the car will start to turn even more sharply, increasing centrifugal force, and so on. Ignoring the cross-wind, the same thing would happen if you actually turned a corner, and in an extreme case the slip angle at the rear would be so much greater than that at the front that the car would spin. And that is what is called oversteer. On the other hand, where the slip angle at the front is greater than that at the rear, a more stable condition of understeer is achieved since, to go back to the cross-wind for a moment, the car tends to turn slightly away from the side thrust, thus creating a centrifugal force in the opposite direction which tend to cancel each other.

ANTI~ROLL BAR

Whether or not a car has basic understeering or oversteering characteristics—or even neither, a condition which is pretty rare called neutral steer—is a matter for the car designer. For instance, understeer can be induced by increasing the proportion of the total weight on the front wheels, while the reverse would increase the oversteering effect. Whatever the car's basic characteristic, however, it can be influenced by a number of methods, which we shall go into a bit later on. Meanwhile, let's have a look at another factor which influences the car's cornering behaviour and roadholding: the roll centre. This is the point in the transverse plane of the suspension about which the sprung mass of the car tends to rotate under the centrifugal force generated by cornering, for instance, the sprung mass of the car being everything, including the driver and passengers, mounted on the springs. The position of the roll-centre on various suspension layouts is quite likely to be different; the typical front wishbone independent system has a relatively low roll-centre compared with the fairly high one found in the normal live-axle rear suspension layout.

Now then. When the sprung mass of the car tends to roll in response to the side forces in cornering, the suspension system functions in such a way that it tends to pull it back up again to its normal upright position, a feature known as roll resistance, or roll stiffness. Where roll stiffness is greater at one end than the other, you find that the stiffer suspension exerts more of this restraining force than that at the other end and there is then a tendency to lift one of the wheels on that axle. Usually, on front-engine-rear-drive cars with "conventional" suspension, it is the rear wheel which will do this, which can cause some embarrassment since some traction is immediately lost. It is therefore a Bad Thing. It is, incidentally, a separate phenomenon to that which causes the back wheels to tramp and patter under fierce acceleration: this is common with the live-axle-semi-elliptic-leaf-spring rear suspension layout, and is due partly to what is called "wind-up" of the springs, and partly to torque reaction which causes a transfer of weight.

With a high-roll-centre, the position of the centre of gravity becomes important. Obviously. it needs to be low, which is why it is common practice to lower the suspension when a car's performance is being improved. But if the roll-centres are high, too low a centre of gravity will tend to delay the breakaway point of the wheels but may make it happen suddenly. With low roll-centres, however, as are found on most i.f.s. cars, this becomes less important, and generally speaking the lower the c. of g. the better.

Body roll itself isn't of any great importance—at least, not necessarily—in its effect on cornering power. Provided the wheels stay firmly on the ground it doesn:t matter very much what the body is doing except that it gets rather uncomfortable inside. An example is the Renault 16, a softly-sprung car with truly outstanding roadholding. Its cornering power, however, is limited not so much by the suspension characteristics in terms of the car's ability to stay on the road as by the high angle of the body roll which makes it difficult for Him to stay in his seat!

From this point of view it is obviously desirable to limit body roll to some extent. We also want to lower the centre of gravity if we can, we want to control wheel-lifting and we want, if possible, to improve the car's stability either by reducing oversteer or increasing understeer, and as well as roll pitching must be reduced. Without re-designing the whole car and altering the whole layout of the suspension system, how can this be done?

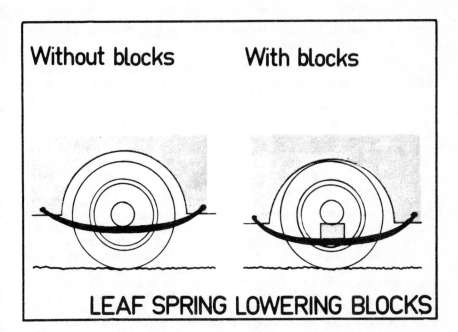

Without blocks

With blocks

LEAF SPRING LOWERING BLOCKS

More than one of these birds can be killed with the same stone, as you might say, and we can put a check on body roll, control wheel-lifting and at the same time increase understeer by fitting an anti-roll bar to the suspension. Cynics have been known to suggest that the function of this item of equipment is to convert independent suspension back to the old beam-axle type, but putting it a little more technically its purpose is to transfer roll resistance from the usually stiffer rear end to the front, thus making the front suspension provide a greater resistance to roll. Increasing the rate of the front springs, or decreasing the rate of those at the back, would have the same effect. It is generally better to achieve the result by fitting a suitable anti-roll bar, however, because, as the bar is only working to its full effect when one front wheel is on maximum bump while the other is on maximum rebound—as, for instance, when the car is cornering close to its limits—it doesn't normally affect any other aspect of the front suspension's workings, and does not, for example, give a harder ride.

Pitch and, to some extent, roll can also be inhibited by stiffening the dampers, or shock absorbers as they are more usually and inexplicably known. The usual purpose of these is to absorb excess spring movement and without them to control the springs the car would bounce up and down like a ping-pong ball. With ineffective dampers, the movement of the sprung mass of the car is uncontrolled and tends to build up to the point at whcih the thing goes clean out of control, which can obviously be a bit naughty. By stiffening them, therefore, we can control the spring movement even more and although they will not actually restrict body movement, they will slow down the rate of such movement. In other words, where dampers are being used to control, say, roll, they don't actually stop the body from moving. What happens is that the car will take longer to assume its complete attitude of roll, so that the cause is removed before the full angle of heel is reached.

The centre of gravity is usually lowered by lowering the car bodily. Where semi-elliptic leaf springs are involved, such as the most common rear suspension lay out, this can be done quite simply by inserting packing pieces or spacers, between the springs themselves and the axle casing. Lowering the c. of g. will clearly make the car more stable in the lateral plane, but where coil spring suspension is used, as on common forms of independent front suspension, the coils themselves must be shortened. It is necessary to tread a little warily here, since altering the spring length can sometimes also alter its rate, and if the spring rate is reduced we can adversely affect the car's understeering qualities: when in doubt, do as the experts do!

We haven't said much yet about wheels and tyres. Here again, it's difficult to say a little without saying a lot, because tyres in particular are a very complex subject which can sometimes be dangerously over-simplified. Generally speaking, improved roadholding could be achieved by replacing the then existing cross-ply tyres with the superior radial-ply covers—presumably there is no need to go too deeply into the reasons for this, but it can be said that the radials impart a smaller slip angle and if you want to think about that, turn back a bit. Even more recent development in terms of low-profile cross-ply tyres may well have made this move either out-of-date of unnecessary, though. The simple answer is to get the expert advice: provided you are explicit about the purpose for which the tyres are to be used, the tyre manufacturers can supply an answer.

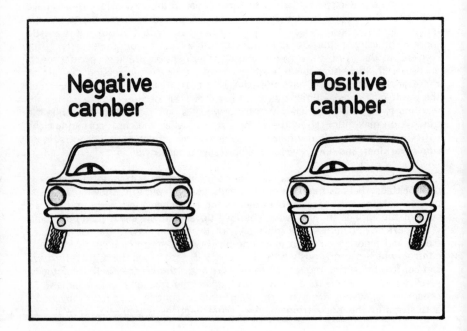

Where you can run into problems is in the currently-fashionable exercise of fitting over-size tyres. These go with wider-than-standard wheel rims and the overall effect is to increase the car's track and widen its base area which will logically bring benefits in terms of lateral stability. But while this may bring about an increase in potential cornering speeds it is worth bearing in mind that these are at best slight for road cars compared with some of the disadvantages. Colin Campbell, in his book, "The Sports Car—Its design and Performance" suggests that a thirty per cent increase in rim width gives a ten per cent increase in cornering power, and more recent developments in tyre tread design and rubber compounds may mean that a good part of this improvement could be achieved by a change of tyre alone.

Be that as it may, an increase in rim width and tyre tread area will improve roadholding. Disadvantages, however, which may be small for cars used in competition when wear and tear on all parts is high, but which may be more serious on a road car include, principally, increased loadings on wheel bearings which will appreciably shorten their life, heavier steering effort, a less comfortable ride and, in some cases, the physical difficulties of incorporating a large-section wheel and tyre inside the wheel arch, especially when the space available for wheel movement has already been reduced by suspension lowering.

Tyre pressure can play a large part in the car's handling, cornering performance and stability, and cornering power increases with inflation pressure to an astonishing amount. Colin Campbell, in his book, has given a table for a typical cross-ply tyre which shows that, with a normal cornering power of 70 lb./degree at normal inflation pressure, the effect of a twenty per cent under-inflation is to reduce this to 56, while a twenty per cent over-inflation increases it to 82.

Thus it can easily be seen that understeer can be emphasised by reducing the front tyre pressure or increasing the rear tyre pressure, the reverse tending to emphasise oversteer. For high-speed motoring, at sustained speeds, it is usual to increase normal inflation pressures by amounts which vary according to the sustained speed likely to be held—the tyre manufacturers can supply this information.

Another factor which plays a large part in stability and understeer/oversteer is the camber of the wheels—that is, the angle to the vertical plane at which they are set. Understeer can be induced by giving the rear wheels negative camber— that is, the wheel leans inwards at the top—while the front wheels retain normal or are even given positive camber; to reduce understeer the rear wheels would be retained in a normal camber attitude while those at the front are given a small amount of negative camber.

We haven't yet mentioned the brakes except in so far as their performance is affected by the suspension. This aspect is a simple one—the brakes cannot do anything about stopping the car, as distinct from stopping the wheel, unless the wheel is in firm contact with the road. But even when it is, it is quite possible that the brakes fitted to the car in standard form will not be able to cope with the increased performance that tuning has achieved. This is almost certainly true of practically every installation and simply because the car has, for instance, disc front brakes, that is no guarantee that the stoppers will be up to the job they have to do when the car is travelling faster. Sustained use of even the standard car's top levels of performance may strain them a bit, while if you have tuned the car for more urge the chances of running into things like brake fade are pretty good.

This problem, luckily, is usually fairly straightforward to deal with. In a good many cases it will only be necessary to modify the brakes by fitting friction material—either the linings of drum brakes of the pads of discs—of a harder grade than standard. As with sparking plugs, which we discussed earlier, the business of hardness and softness has nothing to do with the obvious aspect of friction material, and a "soft" lining doesn't mean you can use it to fill cushions. The material used has, as a basis, some form of asbestos, which, as you know, is remarkably heat-resistant and also has good frictional properties. Usually, the compound is re-inforced with metal—soft metals and alloys in the main, to reduce the amount by which these metal bits score the drums.

The biggest problem in braking is the question of what is called fade, which is what happens when the brakes get good and hot after hard or repeated use and all the braking effort, or at least most of it, disappears: when the brakes have cooled down, it usually returns in full measure and you are back to full stopping power until next time. The reasons for this are somewhat varied and they are nearly all very technical, but one of them which is worth mentioning is a simple matter of expansion. Friction, of course, generates heat, and the amount of friction necessary to stop a motor-car weighing a ton from, say, ninety miles per hour generates aneluvva lotta heat. Every schoolboy and, presumably, schoolgirl knows that when metal is heated, it expands, and most of us also know that different metals expand to a different extent when subjected to similar amounts of heat. With drum brakes, the drums and the shoes (to which the lining material is attached) are made of different metals, they expand at a different rate and the result is that the curvature of the linings no longer matches up with the drums. And bingo, you're no longer stopping like you used to. This problem, obviously, can't arise with disc brakes because there is neither drum nor curved lining, and this is one of the ways in which disc brakes are fundamentally superior to drums: disc brakes can fade, but for different reasons. What is needed for brake linings and pads, therefore, is a material which will dissipate heat as quickly as possible without undergoing any kind of chemical change (such as catching fire, which can and does happen). The brakes themselves must be well-ventilated (another point on which discs are superior, because all their working parts, or all those which get hot, are out in the open air). Fortunately, it is easy to produce material which meets up with these requirements, but less happily such a material has other properties, inevitably, which are less desirable. These materials are knows as "harder" grades; examples, are the Ferodo VG/95 lining and DS11 disc pad material. These provide increased resistance to fade and are therefore suitable for faster cars since they will stop the thing more often from higher speeds without losing their frictional qualities. But they will also demand a higher pedal pressure for a given braking effect, and they will also tend to be less effective when they are cold. For this reason standard motor-cars of the low-performance category aren't given them to start with: they aren't intended to be thrashed around the countryside frequently slowing down from maximum speed, and they are expected to be used a good deal around town where violent braking is rarely necessary and where heavy pedal pressures are certainly undesirable, especially, or so the motor industry thinks, when women are likely to be often driving the car. (The motor industry chivalrously, still regards women as the weaker sex, and if your girl-friend has Girton thighs and a kick like a mule as the result of a life-time of hockey, or mountaineering, or some other gentle feminine enterprise, that has nothing to do with the case).

To overcome this additional pedal pressure, you can fit a servo, which is what is meant by "power-assistance". This device assists the action of the brake pedal by making use of the vacuum, or depression, in the inlet manifold. When you press on the brake pedal a valve opens, applying suction to a piston operating in an air-tight cylinder: the piston nips along the cylinder and gives an additional yank to the brake rod. It is important to bear in mind, though, that this device, clever as it is, doesn't do anything to give you more braking—it merely gives you more braking for a given pedal pressure. In other words, if you get maximum braking effect from a pedal pressure, with no servo assistance, of, say, 40 lb., the servo will enable you to achieve maximum braking for a pedal effort, plus servo, of, say, 30 lb. But the maximum braking effort remains the same.

Apart from disc and drums, brakes themselves fall into various categories, some of which are better for our purpose than others. Two-leading shoe drum brakes are more popular than the leading-trailing shoe arrangement because with two leading-shoes (a shoe is said to be leading when the movement of the drum over the lining is towards the point at which the shoe is pivoted) both shoes tend to be more tightly into contact with the drum by the drums' own movement.

Chapter 6

Transmissions, Body Parts and Instruments

If you have ever tried to pedal uphill on a pushbike fitted with a three-speed hub, or something of the sort, which is in the highest gear, you'll have learnt early in life the advantages of variable gearing. These advantages apply just as strongly to the motor-car as they did to your aching leg-muscles because of the internal combustion engine's limited torque range. Engine speed and road-speed are obviously linked, and if, because of gradient or some other reason, the car slows down to a road speed which means that the engine has to run at a speed below that at which it develops power and torque in useful amounts, you'll want a lower gear, chum. Not only is the engine speed below its peak, but the poor motor is physically trying to lift the car up the hill against the force of gravity, and if you want to know how strong that is, try jumping out of the bedroom window.

What is ideally needed is an infinitely-variable gear ratio, so that whatever the road speed you can maintain a more or less constant engine speed and thus maintain a steady output of power or torque. Unfortunately this isn't practically possible—although the Daf Variomatic transmission comes pretty near. But most cars have to put up with a set a fixed gear-ratios and the driver, either directly, as in the case of a normal manual transmission, or indirectly, as with automatics, has to make up his mind which one will suit him best. He doesn't have a free choice, of course; he can only make his selection, normally, from the ratios the manufacturer has decided will do the best job for the car, and once we have fiddled about with the car and made its performance characteristics totally different from those envisaged back at the factory, it follows that the original set of ratios won't necessarily be as good for the car as they were.

In a good many cases there is something we can do about this, but before we get onto that we'd better look at what we're trying to do. You hear people going on about low gears and high ones, widely-spaced and close-ratio patterns. What's all this about, then? First of all, low ratios allow high engine-speeds compared with low road-speeds—in other words, the engine is whistling around at high rev while the road wheels to which it is indirectly connected are turning slowly. This is the sort of ratio needed for starting.

There are snags in this operation, of course. To begin with, you've got to bear in mind that an alteration to the final-drive ratio will effect a similar alteration on all the overall gear ratios from top to bottom, and although fitting, say, a higher final-drive ratio will certainly give you the higher second gear you wanted, it will also give you a higher bottom gear, which may then be too high for traffic driving, or starting from rest on a hill; you'll get a higher top gear too, which may appear desirable on the face of it since you'll be able to go quicker. But bear in mind, for instance, that what is loosely called wind-resistance increases by roughly the cube of the speed and you can begin to see that an appreciable increase in power is necessary if you are going to be able to make use of a higher top gear.

Compromise is clearly called for. An overall lowering of the gearing will give improved acceleration; an overall raising of the ratios will give, possibly, a slightly higher top speed; it may mean that while the top speed remains unaltered on a level road, the higher speeds available in the lower gears may be of material benefit to overall performance. Small variations can also be observed by changing tyres from one type to another, and most of the major tyre companies can supply figures for the rolling radius of the various sizes of their tyres from which you can calculate the effect such a change will have on the gear ratio.

An important part of the transmission which we haven't yet dealt with is the clutch, which is, of course, the vital link between engine and gearbox. The chances are that if by tuning you have gained a significant increase in power from the engine the clutch will no longer be man enough to transmit the extra urge without slipping and, ultimately, burning out. Here again it may be possible to fit a stronger clutch, either from the list of options supplied by competition-minded manufacturers, or by using a tougher lining material which can be obtained from the friction-material firms. As with brakes, a really strong clutch designed to stand up to competition stresses will call, usually, for a good deal more effort on the clutch pedal, while it may also be of the "in-or-out" type, with a lack of progressive engagement which can be slightly embarrassing in traffic driving.

BODY AND INTERIOR

There is more than one way of killing a cat, so they say (sadistically) and, equally, there is more than one way of getting more performance from a motor-car than the original manufacturers intended. We've discussed getting more power from the engine, but we can also achieve a similar result by giving the engine less to lug about, so that it can devote more of its horses to making the thing go faster. For serious tuning we have to consider both. The obvious way to tackle the job is to do as Colin Chapman used to suggest, and "add lightness" . To do this, you don't go mad with a drill and bore holes in every flat surface, but you can, carefully, replace some of the heavy steel panels with much lighter ones in light alloy or glassfibre. Obvious examples are the boot and bonnet lids, while in some cases - a lot depends on the particular car - you can replace much larger chunks of heavy steel with lightweight material. Provided the panel is not an important stress-bearing member it can, in general, be replaced, but you should be cautious about this. For instance, you might think that the doors are natural subjects for this operation, but remember that glassfibre doors will be a good deal less rigid than the original steel ones, and if you are going to use your car as road transport it might be unpleasant if the door was to flex and fly open.

Most of the windows can be replaced by Perspex instead of the normal heavy glass. Again, remember that Perspex scratches very easily, so we suggest leaving the windscreen in particular out of this particular manoeuvre, or the first time.

SPECIAL STEERING WHEELS

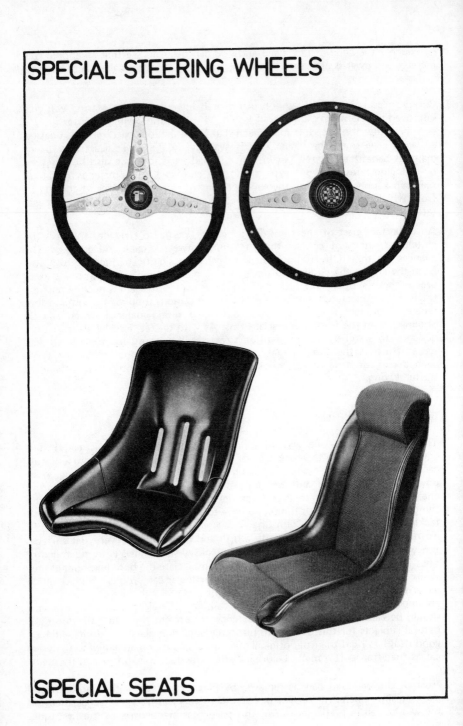

SPECIAL SEATS

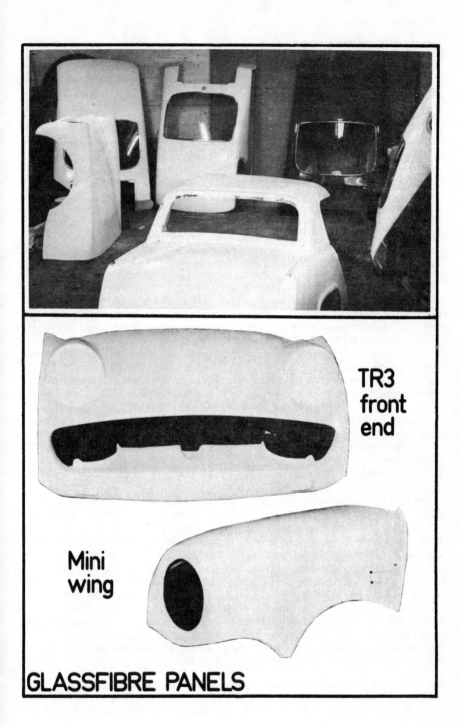

TR3
front
end

Mini
wing

GLASSFIBRE PANELS

Special Dash Panel

you use the screen-wipers you'll find it necessary to replace it. The best bet for the screen is a laminated glass one and this, of course, is compulsory if you are planning on any sort of competition as scrutineers won't permit you to use the usual toughened type.

If you're really being ruthless, you can save more weight by stripping out all the interior trim—door trim-panels, carpets, passenger-seat cushions and so on. This leaves you with a lightish car but one which is a pretty nasty place to sit, so that sort of thing is best left to track racers.

The inside of the car will need a little treatment if you are going to do the job properly on your high-performance mighty motor. The level of instrumentation provided as standard by most manufacturers nowadays falls short of the requirements of the enthusiast with a tuned car, and the average driver's seat can stand a lot of improvement when it comes to fast motoring. And once you've altered that, some of the controls will need modifying, too. Generally, the standard seats provide inadequate support for fast motoring and the poor driver has to hang on using the steering wheel as a sort of grab-handle instead of simply something to steer with.

The thing to do is to swap the standard perch for one of the specially-designed seats which provide support in all the right places, are generally a lot more comfortable for long journeys than the standard ones and which give plenty of wrap-around about the thighs and shoulders to hold you in place when you are cornering hard.

If the cost of these makes you blink, you can think about one of the padded covers which can be fitted to the standard seat: either way, you'll probably want to alter the position of the seat mountings to give a better, more comfortable driving position. When you've done this, you might not be able to reach the gearlever properly—probably, you couldn't before, come to that, so you can fit an extension piece which may be cranked back to bring the knob into a better position. The steering wheel, too, can be changed. Many of the ones fitted as standard are larger than they need be, and by changing to a smaller diameter—about 13 ins. is usually the most comfortable—you will give yourself more knee-room, if the car is one of the Mini range it'll mean you can fit a column-adjusting bracket to bring the wheel more nearly into the vertical plane, and while you're on the changing kick you can select one of those with a padded, leather-covered rim for greater comfort and much more positive control.

Once we start pressing-on a bit we find the heel-and-toe gearchange a bit of a help, usually: if you don't know what this is, it's a means of operating the brake pedal with the ball of your foot and the throttle pedal with the side of it, simultaneously. This means you can make the actions of braking and changing down for a corner happen together and the car is kept under control and more stable by doing so. Why is it called heel-and-toe? Because the first chaps to start doing it were driving cars which, as was common in those days, had the loud pedal in the middle instead of on the right, and you jabbed your toe on the brake and your heel on the throttle. But the modern pedal arrangement prevents this—unless you have somewhat unusual ankles. Anyway, some cars have their pedals so placed in relation to each other that it is impossible, but you can put this right quite simply by attaching a piece of metal to the throttle pedal.

Then instruments. The ones supplied by the average motor manufacturer nowadays consist of speedometer, a fuel contents gauge and, if you're dead lucky, a thermometer as well. This may be alright for some but it falls a bit short for our requirements because we like to know what's going on as much as possible and because we also have the sense to interpret the information which additional dials can give us, unlike the average peasant who would simply be confused.

Top of the list of our requirements is the rev-counter, or tachometer. The most popular choice is one which works on the electronic principle, designed to be connected to the low-tension side of the ignition circuit and recording engine revolutions by counting the number of pulses in the ignition system. Then you'll want an oil-pressure gauge, a water temperature gauge if the maker didn't provide one, and if your really fussy an oil-temperature gauge as well. These all replace warning lights which to be honest don't do much good until the trouble has happened, whereas the gauge can tell the observant driver—no use having a lot of dials if you don't look at 'em, is it?—that trouble is happening and gives him a chance to do something about it before it's too late. Over and above these, an ammeter is handy: the ignition warning light isn't quite as useless as, say, the oil-pressure warning light, but it is certainly not as useful as a proper ammeter. Accessory suppliers can supply additional supplementary instrument panels for these items, unless you prefer to try and accomodate them in the normal dashboard or a full-width replacement.

All this more or less sums up the groundwork to tuning. We haven't been able to go into much detail, but have concentrated on trying to explain the principles behind the detail, which is really the next lesson, as you might say. We'll wind up, therefore, with a few formulae and calculations which you might find useful.

USEFUL FORMULAE

To find the swept volume V of single cylinder:
$$V = \frac{3.14 \times D^2 \times S}{4}$$
where D = cylinder bore; S = stroke.

To find the compression ratio CR:
$$CR = \frac{V + v}{v}$$
where V = swept volume and v = volume of space above piston at top of stroke (*total* volume of cumbustion chamber).

To find the brake horse power bhp:
$$bhp = \frac{PLAN}{33,000},$$ where P —brake mean effective pressure in lb./sq. ins;

L —length of stroke in feet
A —area of piston in square inches
N —number of power strokes/ minute

Alternatively:
$$bhp = \frac{r.p.m. \times torque\ in\ lb/ft}{5250}$$

Brake mean effective pressure (in lb./sq.ins.) $= \frac{bhp \times 3300}{LAN}$

where L —length of stroke in feet
A —area of piston in sq. ins.
N —number of power strokes/ minute

To find the torque:
$$Torque = \frac{bhp \times 5250}{r.p.m.}$$

Alternatively:
$$Torque = \frac{PV}{4\pi} \text{ lb. in.}$$

or alternatively
$$Torque = \frac{PV}{4\pi \times 12} \text{ lb. ft.}$$ where P —brake mean effective pressure in lb./sq.ins. V—swept volume in cu. ins.

To find speed in m.p.h.;
$$m.p.h. = \frac{r.p.m. \times wheel\ diam.\ in\ inches}{gear\ ratio \times 336}$$

speed sport motobooks

THE PERFORMANCE PAPERBACKS

INTERAUTO

A NEW SERIES
of
AUTO ENGINEERING
REFERENCE BOOKS

The following pages present to you some of the
current SpeedSport and Interauto books for the
motoring enthusiast, the automobile technician
and the motorist.

Motorsport

HOW TO START MOTOR RACING. Wally Hall. 011.9.

The author has had considerable club racing success and has passed on most of the vast experience he has gained. Ideal for anyone at all interested in beginning.

HOW TO START RALLYING. Colin Malkin. 024.0.

This famous rally driver takes the reader through all the mystiques of rally preparation. Car selection, suitability and setting up. Bodywork, lights, driving and navigation are some of the subjects dealt with. Colin co-drove the winning London to Sydney Marathon car.

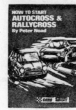

HOW TO START AUTOCROSS AND RALLYCROSS. Peter Noad. 033.X.

Like the rest of the 'How to Start' series but for the increasingly popular sport of autocross/rallycross. Like the other authors Peter Noad is an experienced and successful campaigner.

MOTORCYCLE ENGINEERING 075-5 £2.25 Phil Irving

'Phil' Irving — motorcycle designer, engineer, rider, and, as 'Slide Rule', one of the best-known technical writers on motorcycling — established his reputation as a rider After the war, as Vincent's Chief Engineer, he designed and developed the Series B 'Rapide' with its renowned variants. He has designed a six-litre diesel engine for an Australian tractor and is at present engaged in the development of racing cars and high-performance equipment.

HOW TO START PRODUCTION MOTOR CYCLE RACING 030.5

Ray Knight
Ray Knight is a journalist with 10 years racing, a TT win and lap record to his credit. He passes all his experience to the enthusiast. 'A good guide to success.

THE *BARRY LEE* BOOK OF HOT ROD RACING   062.3

Barry Lee revolutionised Hot Rod Racing in 1970 and in 1971 became British Champion, as well as making successful forays to Denmark and South Africa. In his book Barry Lee shows how he built his Escort, what it's like in a hot rod race, where and when hot rod racing takes place - in fact he writes about everything that an intending competitor, a hot rod fan or spectator will want to know.

Marque tuning guides

TUNING THE MINI. Clive Trickey   001.0.
The Mini Tuners' Bible; universally recognised as the most authoritative book on the subject. The most popular marque tuning book to be published.

MORE MINI TUNING. Clive Trickey   000.3.
New! The second edition of the companion volume to 'Tuning the Mini'. Updated with much more information on valve gear, carbs, camshafts and gearboxes.

TUNING STANDARD TRIUMPHS over 1300 cc.   029.1.
David Vizard
The tuning stages for Vitesses, GT6, TRs and all 2000 units from stage 1 to full race.

TUNING STANDARD TRIUMPHS up to 1300 cc.   012.7.
Richard Hudson-Evans
Essential reading for Herald, Spitfire, 1300, Standard 8 and 10 owners. Full tuning information.

TUNING VOLKSWAGENS.   Peter Noad   026.7.
An expert guide to the race and rally preparations of VWs; it covers the various types of car and their development and competition history. Includes a section on Beach Buggies.

TUNING ESCORTS AND CAPRIS.   David Vizard   009.7.
The technical editor of 'Cars and Car Conversions' explains engine and chassis tuning procedures for both road and track.

TUNING ANGLIAS AND CORTINAS. 003.8.

This bestseller deals with engine and chassis tuning and details the early Classic and Capri, the V4 and Twin Cam power units.

TUNING TWIN CAM FORDS. David Vizard 007.0.

The stage-by-stage modifications for these engines, from 'warm' 1600s to full-race 1800s. Fully illustrated.

TUNING FOUR CYLINDER FORDS. Paul Davies. 059.3.

A new edition of this very popular tuning bible for all four cylinder models from Anglia to Cortina MK III.

TUNING BMC SPORTS CARS. Mike Garton 004.6.

The author, once a technical expert at British Leyland Special Tuning Department passes his wealth of experience on to the interested owner.

TUNING VIVAS AND FIRENZAS Blydenstein & Coburn 064.X

Written by the country's leading experts, this is the first tuning book on these popular cars. It covers all aspects of tuning for both road and track.

TUNING V8 ENGINES. David Vizard 028.3.

This book covers the principles involved for modifying a large selection of V8 engines— design trends, supercharging, assembly, part swapping, carburation etc.

TUNING COMPANION SERIES

TUNING LUCAS IGNITION SYSTEMS   063.1

This book examines each component in the Lucas ignition system
and explains how to test and check that it is functioning correctly.
Also dealt with are the special procedures and requirements of
systems on high performance engines, with setting up instructions,
trouble shooting hints and comprehensive data tables.

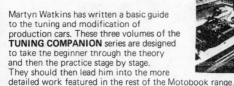

Martyn Watkins has written a basic guide
to the tuning and modification of
production cars. These three volumes of the
TUNING COMPANION series are designed
to take the beginner through the theory
and then the practice stage by stage.
They should then lead him into the more
detailed work featured in the rest of the Motobook range.

INTRODUCTION TO TUNING   002.X.
ENGINES AND TRANSMISSIONS   013.5
SUSPENSIONS AND BRAKES   027.5

AUTO ELECTRICS.   **David Westgate.**   **014.3.**
A well illustrated and easily readable guide to the car's electrical system.
This book should be a standard work as it covers all aspects of this
complicated subject from batteries to ammeters.

CAR CUSTOMISING.   **Paul Cockburn.**   **031.3.**
A new book on this increasingly popular form of car modification.
Paul Cockburn a brilliant young designer explains the ground work and
suggests many practical ideas.

MODIFYING PRODUCTION CYLINDER HEADS.
Clive Trickey.   **008.9.**
Clive Trickey's famous basic guide to the modification of cylinder heads for
improved performance. A standard work which has become a best seller.

RACING ENGINE PREPARATION.   **Clive Trickey.**   **015.1.**
Fully describes the conversion of mass-produced engines to full blown
racing units.

New edition
Castrol Book of Car Care

SBN 902-587-005

This is the new edition of the ever popular Castrol Book of Car Care in a new format and at a new price.

'Car Care' has been rewritten and considerably updated, with new drawings, diagrams and photographs. It now has a full-colour cover.

'Car Care' does exactly what its title suggests under the following chapter headings:

1. A Happy Partnership? 2. Servicing; 3. Bodywork; 4. Engine; 5. Transmission; 6. Brakes; 7. Suspension and Steering; 8. Tyres; 9. Electrics; 10. Breakdown Trouble-shooter; 11. Safety and Security; 12. Castrol at your Service.

The Big Drive

THE BIG DRIVE.
Richard Hudson-Evans and Graham Robson.
032.1.
The Book of the World Cup Rally, 1970.
The first behind-the-wheel view of the toughest rally ever—the car breaking London, to Mexico Race.

Castrol Book of Motor Cycle Care

a sister publication to the **'Castrol Book of Car Care'** describes the various parts of the machine tells what they are designed to do and suggests the best course of action for looking after them. Used intelligently it can save a lot of time, money and frustration.

Still very popular and a constant best seller.

SU CARBURETTERS
ISBN: 0-903192-25-X
110 pages

One of the most informative books ever published on this popular make of carburetter. Models included are the 'H', 'HD', 'HS', 'HS8', Thermo and MC2. Extensive coverage is given to the maintenance overhaul and tuning of the SU carburetter. Also included is an application section giving carburetter details relating to vehicle make and model.
CONTENTS: Carburetter Duty — Engine Requirements — Influence of Induction Systems — SU Carburetter — Dismantling — Overhaul — Tuning — Adjusting — Servicing — Application tables, needle size charts.

STROMBERG CARBURETTERS
ISBN: 0-903192-52-7
152 pages

Full information and details of operation, testing procedure, tuning and maintenance of the Stromberg CD range of carburetters for internal combustion automobile and marine engines.

SOLEX CARBURETTERS
ISBN: 0-903192-09-8
158 pages

An informative guide with coverage of servicing, function, testing, overhauls and adjustments of French Solex models used in Citroens, Peugeots, Renaults and Simcas. With extensive data and many diagrams.

ZENITH CARBURETTERS
ISBN: 0-903192-39-X
148 pages

Like the other books in the series, gives full advice on maintenance and tells how to get the best out of your Zenith Carburetter.

Workshop Series

A range of books on important but much-neglected aspects of automotive technology for the engineer and mechanic.

PETROL FUEL INJECTION SYSTEMS

ISBN: 0-903192-20-9
Size: 8½" x 11"
380 pages Illustrated

One of the first books published containing detailed information on the construction and operation of most of the major petrol fuel injection systems available today. The opening section deals with the development of the first P.I. Systems, dating as far back as 1940. This is followed by descriptive information and technical data on various systems available on the

present day market. Finally, service information on a number of vehicles to which a P.I. System has been fitted.

With an abundance of clearly laid-out photographs, drawings and plans, and in the same large format as the other titles in the series, this book covers: AE BRICO, BOSCH(Mechanical and Electronic), KUGEL-FISHER, LUCAS & TECALEMIT in relation to the motor vehicles equipped with these systems.

ALTERNATOR SERVICE MANUAL

ISBN: 0-903192-28-4
Size: 8½" x 11"
250 pages Illustrated

This valuable publication for automotive electricians deals extensively with the testing and maintenance of Alternators and Regulators. Compiled from genuine manufacturers' service manuals.

CONTENTS: Alternator technology Bosch, Butec, CAV, Chrysler, Delco, Remy, Email, Fiat, Ford. Hitachi, Leece-Neville, Lucas, Mitsubishi. Motorola & Prestolite Application tables listing current vehicles and their standard alternators, for easy cross reference.

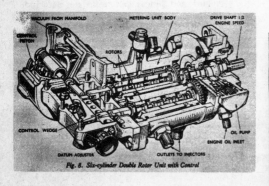

Fig. 8. Six-cylinder Double Rotor Unit with Control

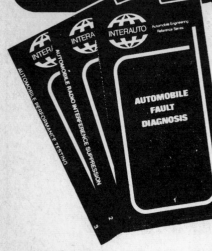

AUTOMOBILE BODY AND PAINTWORK REPAIRS
ISBN: 0-903192-04-7   110 pages
A concise and up-to-the-minute book dealing
with a difficult and frequently under-estimated
'art'. Extensive descriptions are furnished on
the various body straightening machines, welding
and body finish. Also included is a section on
fibreglass bodies. All body and paint repair shops
will find this publication immensely helpful.
CONTENTS: Planning — Body Repairs — Body
and Frame Straighteners — Straightening
Techniques — Body Jigs — Body Repair Tools —
Panel Beating Work — Welding — Paint Finish —
Paintshop — Spraying Equipment — Paint Build-up.

Fig. 22 and 23 — Wheel alignment, using Projektus method

A sample page from Automobile Fault Diagnosis

AUTOMOBILE ENGINE TESTING
ISBN: 0-903192-03-9   140 pages
This publication deals with the subject of engine testing from all aspects. It
includes basic test operations, the use of sophisticated test equipment and the
operation of diagnostic test bays. In all senses, this is a compact and informative
work providing up-to-date knowledge on a vital topic. It also incorporates
extensive fault-finding charts.
CONTENTS: Basic Testing — Battery Test — Spark Plug Test — Compression Test
— Contact Breaker Test — Ignition Timing — Ignition Test — Condenser Test —
Suppression Test — Engine Test — Cylinder Balancing — Feed Pump Test —
Carburetter Adjustment — Exhaust Check — Generator Test — Test Equipment.

AUTOMOBILE FAULT DIAGNOSIS
ISBN: 0-903192-24-1   120 pages
Covers the basic fault diagnosis, repair and adjustment of motor vehicles based on
current practices and equipment. Also includes fault-finding charts.
CONTENTS: Faults on the Engine — Cooling System — Lubrication System —
Fuel System — Cylinders — Pistons — Rings and Connecting Rods — Crankshaft
and Flywheel — Valve-Gear — Inlet and Exhaust Systems — Chassis — Clutch —
Gearbox — Final Drive — Steering and Front Axle — Fibre Glass Bodies.

AUTOMOBILE PERFORMANCE TESTING
ISBN: 0-903192-07-1   150 pages
This is a companion volume to 'Automobile Engine Testing', giving equally exten-
sive coverage to the subject of stationary and dynamic test methods for motor
vehicles. The construction, function and operation of dynomometers and other
vehicle test equipment is examined in detail.
CONTENTS: Function — Performance — Static Tests — Road Test —
Dynomometer Tests — Fault-Finding.

AUTOMOBILE RADIO INTERFERENCE SUPPRESSION
ISBN: 0-903192-02-0   110 pages
An authoritative work describing the propogation of electrical interference and
the various methods of suppression.
CONTENTS: Radios in Motor Vehicles — Radio Reception — Car Aerials — Radio
Interference — Types of Suppression — Testing Close Range Interference Suppress-
ion — Extensive Fault-Finding Chart.

BOSCH ELECTRICAL SYSTEMS
ISBN 0-903192-06-3   184 pages
Not a purely theoretical write-up on Bosch Electrical Systems but a practical
pocket guide for those concerned with working on them. The reader will find that
in a very brief but extremely comprehensive way all the testing, trouble-shooting,
servicing and repair instructions are given that are really required. A major feature
of this book is the way in which it will help to diagnose faults rapidly and system-
atically.
Includes details of: Circuit Diagrams, Wiring Looms, Lighting Systems, Signalling
Devices, Batteries, Generators, Coils, Spark Plugs, Starter Motors.

HOW TO ORDER
Motobooks

Whenever you wish to purchase any of the listed books take this form to your Bookseller or Motorshop who will order the book for you. If this is not possible, mail the order form to us with your payment and we will send the required books to you by return.

Please observe the following instructions:

ORDERING BOOKS BY MAIL	from	ALBION SCOTT LTD. Bercourt House 51 York Road Brentford Middx TW8 OQP England

Identify required books on this form.
Mail complete form to us, with your remittance (either cheque, postal order or cash) to which you must add the postage as set out below.

Make sure that your
NAME and ADDRESS is given in the space below.

Postage and Packing:

Book price to		UK	EUROPE	OVERSEAS
	£2.00	10p	15p	20p
	£3.00	15p	20p	25p
over	£3.00	20p	30p	40p

Dispatch by surface book mail only.

Name ....

Address ....

Special Instructions ....

Get your facts straight from a Motobook

SPECIAL TITLES FROM ALBION SCOTT

Qty.	Title	Price	Total
	SPEEDSPORT		
	Tuning SU Carburetters	£1.00	
	Tuning Weber, Vol. 1	70p	
	Tuning Weber, Vol. 2	£1.00	
	Tuning Stromberg Carbs.	50p	
	Tuning Solex Carburetters	£1.30	
	Tuning Zenith Carburetters	£1.00	
	Tuning the Mini	£1.20	
	More Mini Tuning	£1.30	
	Tuning Four Cyl. Fords	£1.50	
	Tuning Anglias and Cortinas	£1.00	
	Tuning Twin Cam Fords	£1.00	
	Tuning Escorts and Capris	£1.00	
	Tuning Vivas & Firenzas	£1.30	
	Tuning BMC Sports Cars	£1.00	
	Triumphs to 1300 cc	70p	
	Tuning Triumphs over 1300 cc	£1.60	
	Tuning the VW	£1.50	
	Tuning V8 Engines	£1.80	
	How to Start Rallying	£1.00	
	Barry Lee Hot Rod	£1.00	
	How to Start Motor Racing	£1.00	
	How to Start Autocross	£1.00	
	Prod. Motorcy. Racing	£1.00	
	Introduction to Tuning	70p	
	Engines and Transm.	70p	
	Suspensions and Brakes	70p	
	Auto Electrics	£1.50	
	Lucas Ignition Systems	£1.00	
	Modif. Prod. Cy. Heads	70p	
	Racing Engine Prep.	£1.20	
	Car Customising	£1.00	
	High Speed Driving	£1.50	
	Cylinder Head Modific.	£1.50	
	Chassis Tuning	£1.50	
	Motorcycle Engineering	£2.25	
	The Big Drive	50p	
	Castrol Book of Car Care	25p	
	Motorcycle Care	25p	
	Qty TOTAL Price		

Qty.	Title	Price	Total
	INTERAUTO		
	Fault Diagnosis	£1.15	
	Interference Suppression	£1.15	
	Body and Paintwork	£1.15	
	Performance Testing	£1.15	
	Engine Testing	£1.15	
	Bosch Electrical Systems	£1.15	
	Caravan Service Manual	£1.15	
	SU Carburetters	£1.15	
	Solex Carburetters (Vol. 1)	£1.15	
	Zenith Carburetters	£1.15	
	Stromberg Carburetters	£1.15	
	Alternator Manual	£3.00	
	Petrol Fuel Injection	£4.50	
	CRYPTON		
	Engine and Electrical	£3.00	
	Corrective Service	£2.50	
	Diagnostic Wallchart	£2.50	
	WORKSHOP MANUALS		
	quote make, model & year		
	Cars	£2.50	
	Motorcycles	£2.00	
	HANDBOOKS		
	quote make, model & year	75p	
	Motorist Emergency Signs	75p	
	Motobook Catalogue	20p	
	Qty TOTAL Price		

NOTES

Albion Scott Ltd., 51 York Road, Brentford, Middlesex, TW8 0QP
England